A Compact Study of Leviticus

A Compact Study of Leviticus

William T. Miller

WIPF & STOCK · Eugene, Oregon

A COMPACT STUDY OF LEVITICUS

Copyright © 2016 William T. Miller. All rights reserved. Except for brief quotations in critical publications or reviews, no part of this book may be reproduced in any manner without prior written permission from the publisher. Write: Permissions, Wipf and Stock Publishers, 199 W. 8th Ave., Suite 3, Eugene, OR 97401.

Wipf & Stock
An Imprint of Wipf and Stock Publishers
199 W. 8th Ave., Suite 3
Eugene, OR 97401

www.wipfandstock.com

PAPERBACK ISBN 13: 978-1-4982-3367-5
HARDCOVER ISBN 13: 978-1-4982-3369-9

Manufactured in the U.S.A.   01/22/2016

For three women close to the family:
Joan Blyth, Diane Flanel Piniaris, and Sally Poole, OTD.
All demanding of themselves in their careers,
and notably generous and supportive of their families and friends.

Contents

General Introduction to Leviticus • ix
Instructions for Study Groups • xix

Leviticus 1:1—10:20

Section One: Leviticus 1:1—17 • 3
Section Two: Leviticus 2:1-16 • 8
Section Three: Leviticus 3:1-17 • 12
Section Four: Leviticus 4:1-35 • 15
Section Five: Leviticus 5:1-13 • 21
Section Six: Leviticus 5:14—6:7 • 24
Section Seven: Leviticus 6:8—7:38 • 28
Section Eight: Leviticus 8:1-36 • 32
Section Nine: Leviticus 9:1-24 • 36
Section Ten: Leviticus 10:1-20 • 39

Leviticus 11:1—16:54

Section Eleven: Leviticus 11:1—15:33 • 47
Section Twelve: Leviticus 16:1-34 • 64

Leviticus 17:1—27:34

Section Thirteen: Leviticus 17:1-16 • 75
Section Fourteen: Leviticus 18:1-30 • 84
Section Fifteen: Leviticus 19:1-37 • 96
Section Sixteen: Leviticus 20:1-27 • 113
Section Seventeen: Leviticus 21:1—22:33 • 121
Section Eighteen: Leviticus 23:1-44 • 128

Section Nineteen: Leviticus 24:1–23 • 138
Section Twenty: Leviticus 25:1–55 • 147
Section Twenty-One: Leviticus 26:1–46 • 157
Section Twenty-Two: Leviticus 27:1–34 • 165
Final Overview • 169

Answers • 173

Bibliography • 203

General Introduction to Leviticus

I have heard of individual Christians who at some early stage in their religious journeys decide to read the entire Bible cover to cover, unaided. A rule of thumb for such a reading plan is that, by plowing through three chapters a day, it will take one about a year to reach this goal. Some books of the Bible, such as Genesis and Exodus, could give some support to a determined individual who wants to march along with the descendants of Adam and Eve, and Abraham and Sarah. Many other books, however, were not designed to be read in such a methodical, three-chapters-a-day manner. For example, books like Leviticus and much of Numbers and Deuteronomy contain many rules and regulations and very little explanations or even hints as to the origin or the goal of these directives. A novice reader on his or her own would surely wind up with very little comprehension of the rules or of the main goal—learning more about God's love for us and how to live our lives in holiness in tribute to him.

Instead, individuals or groups should look for a guided tour, a slower approach that sheds more light on how complex the biblical writings are—writings influenced by neighboring Ancient Near Eastern and early Western cultures, by changes in thinking over time for ancient Jews and Christians themselves, and by the literary artistry, emotions, and deep faith of those who came before us. To learn more about God's love and will for us we must appreciate the people who wrote and used these books as much as we appreciate the actual contents of the books.

I assume readers coming to Leviticus already have some feel for the flow of events in Genesis and Exodus. The story line of wandering in the desert then continues from Num 10:11 through Deuteronomy. The rules in Leviticus and Num 1:1–10:10 are depicted as a massive set of divine directives handed down from God directly to Moses, the unique lawgiver chosen to build up a people by means of this storehouse or encyclopedia of rubrics and jurisprudence. Some of these laws could not

General Introduction to Leviticus

be immediately used by the exiles, who would have to atone for their sins by forty years of isolation and supervised wandering through the wilderness.

We readers are called upon to understand how this storehouse could have made sense to our ancestors. Only then can we adapt and apply the underlying principles in our worship and in our just dealings with everyone.

I have divided Leviticus into twenty-two *sections*, many the length of a single chapter or two. The five chapters on things that render one ritually unclean (Lev 11–15) are combined into one longer unit. Each section contains basic information that might be useful to have at the start. I do mention fine points of Hebrew vocabulary at times, since Hebrew is so unlike English and has far fewer synonyms. I hope that readers who know biblical Hebrew will allow for my oversimplifications in transcribing these words into English letters. In any case, the basic information should not hinder readers from moving to the consecutively numbered *questions*. These are often scattered through a section by content or put at the very front to elicit initial impressions. They should be studied and answered by individuals or study groups before reference to the *answers* in the back of the book. The *conclusion* to each section is meant to tie up loose ends; a few sections do not need such closing comments.

The plan is that working through the book in this way can contribute to a cohesive guided tour or virtual classroom experience. I hope that my own interest in providing so much information for general readers will not prove daunting or counterproductive. Readers should scan or skip technical segments (but not the Questions) so as not to lose their sense of progress throughout the task.

In the book of Leviticus (with the possible exception of 25:32–34) all the men of the tribe of Levi are considered to be priests. Following the story line from Exodus, the people do not travel during the time covered in Leviticus. Thus there is no need to describe the divinely appointed work forces needed to frequently strike and move the portable tabernacle, as will be recounted in Numbers. In that book one clan of Levi has full priestly status while the other clans have a lesser role as assistants to the priests. Those assistants are called levites. Roman Catholics have a somewhat parallel division of status for priests and deacons, while other Christian denominations use other terms for their classifications of ministers.

General Introduction to Leviticus

A few passages in Leviticus focus on regulations for priests (6:1–7:21; 10:8–15; 16:2–28). Most of the book provides information intended for the entire people of Israel, including the fine points of most religious rituals.

Readers should be aware (and probably are already) of the research regarding the complex editorial layers within the different books of the Pentateuch. Theories about the main editorial layers are still useful, although scholars are more careful now about making absolute claims for these working models. One can still look for the Yahwist (J) and Elohist (E) layers, generally taken as older traditions from the Southern and Northern kingdoms respectively. Many commentators simply refer to a combined JE level, without trying to isolate E verses by themselves. These J and E traditions prevail in much of Genesis and Exodus, and in Numbers starting at 10:11.

The Deuteronomist (D) level enriched not only the Pentateuch but also the historical and prophetic books. Some of that theology is clearly pre-exilic. The D level focuses on sin and repentance, law, covenant, and the promised land. D is in support of David's establishment of the temple in Jerusalem as the primary official shrine for the whole nation. The Deuteronomists argue that this was God's plan from the time of Moses.

Priestly (P) traditions were probably assembled during and after the exile. These traditions focus on the corporate dimensions of God's relationship to the whole world and to the nation of Israel. They preserve details of genealogies, censuses, itineraries, and the rituals of the liturgical year. They made efforts to arrange traditions in chronological order, although they did not have all the evidence needed to be completely successful in this.

P materials prevail in Exod 25–31; 35–40, Leviticus, and Num 1–10. Scholars are more cautious now in picturing Priestly editors as always being the final editors of our biblical books. Sometimes the final editors are simply unknown to us.

While scholars assume that the book of Leviticus comes from Priestly schools, it is obvious that the concerns of the P level about ceremonies in chs. 1–16 are not quite the same as those found in the more general rules of chs. 17–27. The latter block of chapters is commonly called the Holiness Code, and those editors (probably priests also) are given the designation H. At times there is evidence of a second level of editing in and across each of the blocks (designated P2 or H2).

General Introduction to Leviticus

For many details in Leviticus I will rely on the masterful scholarship in the three volumes of Jacob Milgrom's Anchor Bible commentary on Leviticus. Since I do make extensive use of Milgrom's insights, mainly in summary or in paraphrase or at individual verses, I am grateful to Yale University Press, the current owner of the Anchor Bible copyright, for permission to use Milgrom's work in this way specifically for this study guide. I am, of course, responsible for any mistakes in presentation.

Milgrom is convinced that most of the material in Leviticus should be dated from the early to middle eighth century BCE. His argument for this somewhat early pre-exilic date is based on changes that take place in P vocabulary after the exile. As he itemizes examples of these changes in vocabulary, Milgrom counters traditional arguments that much of P is post-exilic. While I do not consider myself skilled in the matter of dating biblical texts, I must grant that Milgrom gives extensive data for his thesis.

One case for the antiquity of P can be found in Ezek 44:8–16. This passage refers to serious incidents that led to some priests being permanently demoted to a lower level of service at the temple. Ezekiel's remarks could be closely linked to Num 18, where levites are clearly assigned to these lower duties for all time. If this is so, then Num 18 cannot be post-exilic in its origins.

Milgrom is also convinced that the H editors redacted P material that was slightly older than H. At times new laws are placed close to the old ones they are changing. Milgrom characterizes P material in Lev 1–16 as very precise in its vocabulary, but often not couched in a style to motivate readers. By contrast, the H level is much less precise in its choice of vocabulary but more motivational, with its focus on the artistic and ethical. Milgrom describes the concerns of the P level as holiness of worship space, mainly involving priests, altars, and sacrifices. The H level has a wider image of holiness, involving everyone in their daily lives, and stresses that God is concerned for the entire promised land, not simply for the tabernacle or temple itself. A good example of the style of H can be found in Lev 21–22. God talks about sanctifying his priests (21:8, 15, 23; 22:9, 16) and about sanctifying all his people (21:8; 22:32). If one were to scan the two blocks in succession (chs. 1–16 and 17–27), the wider interests of H would be noticeable; see ch.17 (meat preparation blood restrictions for resident aliens as well as Israelites), chs. 18 and 20 (sexual prohibitions), ch. 24 (points about blasphemy and murder), ch.

25 (Sabbath years and jubilees), and especially ch. 19 (a profile of what I will call a "utopia of holiness").

Despite the fact that contributing priests and editors might not always have agreed on exact points, they do see the unity between worship ceremonies and the moral and ethical life of the people. One example is Lev 16:20–22, where the atonement ceremonies for the major sins of the nation include a goat that is released in a wilderness area at the end. The certain but lonely demise of the domesticated animal by accident or attack by predators effectively represents the consequences of life without repentance.

In the Pentateuch some biblical regulations simply contradict each other, and those inconsistencies were not resolved in the texts we have received. One example is where and when domestic cattle, sheep, and goats can be slaughtered for major family meals (perhaps only a few times a year). The P tradition has no strict regulation, but H limits the act of slaughtering to shrine sites (Lev 3:16–17; 17:3–7). Deuteronomists follow the P tradition (Deut 12:15, 21), since after the shrines were closed it would have been completely impractical to have ordinary slaughter for meals take place only in Jerusalem.

Milgrom notes that we should consider the importance of Shiloh, the most centrally located of the old shrines. He suggests that some of the logic in Leviticus about sacrifice, portions of sacrifice set aside for priests, examination of people with skin conditions, and lines of priestly succession may now be a combination of practices at Shiloh and at Jerusalem. He notes that Eli, the well-known priest at Shiloh, is considered to be a direct descendant of Aaron of the exodus generation (1 Sam 2:27–28). In another citation he is considered a descendant of Ithamar, Aaron's son (1 Chr 24:3). Eli's line was later discredited, but the new line of Zadokite priests traced their links to Aaron back through Phineas, Aaron's grandson (Num 25:10–13). In noting these two traditions that involve Eli, Milgrom argues against scholarly suggestions that the priestly traditions claiming Aaron as their founder may have been quite late. We may return to some of these points of history during the course of our study.

Turning to some of the theological thinking within the book, Milgrom reminds us that many other Ancient Near Eastern religions took defensive postures about their own temples, frequently devising spells or rites to placate or even control angry gods or demons who might try to desecrate these sacred spaces. In monotheistic Judaism it must be human sinners who defy the LORD and hurt other people, rather than rival gods or demons (which are discounted). Thus ritual impurity often comes from human wrongdoing, and repentance is the main cure in these cases.

The restrictions on those who are currently *unclean* means that they cannot attend services at the tabernacle or temple until they fulfill certain requirements, such as being examined by priests, or undergoing some other purification rite or the passage of a set amount of time. We could use a milder term such as *ineligible* rather than *unclean*, but in any case we must make it clear that these restrictions are not due to any deliberate human sins.

The three main causes of uncleanness are contact with a corpse for any reason, skin eruptions that are white in color, and some genital secretions or bleeding. If we think of these cases as somehow representing dimensions of sin or death, we must remember that they are not demonic forces in themselves. Likewise, the distinctions behind clean and unclean foods may have developed for a variety of reasons, and most likely represent some of the same dimensions of sin or death. The rules for dressing meat and not slaughtering many wild species focus mainly on the proper avoidance and disposition of the blood, which was considered the essential life force. These distinctions about blood and about what is clean and unclean formed a devotional image system honoring God and the life forces he pours out upon us so lavishly.

Beside the food restrictions and the eligibility rules for attendance at the tabernacle, readers are introduced to a bewildering array of mandated and optional sacrifices throughout the liturgical year. No one theory can explain the range of sacrifices that developed within Judaism. Milgrom notes that "the sacrifices cover the gamut of the psychological, emotional, and religious needs of the people." We will need to study each category of sacrifice separately. Some of them were designed to promote true repentance for real sins, and restitution for injustices was an integral part of those ceremonies. Yom Kippur was and remains the paramount annual acknowledgment of the sins of the nation. Milgrom refers to the various rites for purification and atonement as an "ecology of morality."

Another concern was to have a range of alternative items to sacrifice, so that the very poor were on level ground with everyone else. In his book *Judaism: Practice and Belief 63 BCE–66 CE*, E. P. Sanders (p. 112–16) has us imagine a typical Israelite family during the time of Jesus as they make their annual pilgrimage to Jerusalem (not at Passover, in this case). They are a family of average means, and so could only make one trip each year. The husband intends to offer a ram to atone for an earlier unjust small business dealing with a neighbor. He had already repaid the debt with the 20-percent surcharge required by Jewish custom. His wife will offer two doves as a purification rite for herself after the recent birth of their latest child. She had already been purified for assisting at burial customs for a close relative, an uncle. The family will also obtain a lamb for a well-being offering. They will receive much of the meat from that offering to share with family and friends the same day.

Sanders skillfully depicts the family's lived religious or sacramental emotions accompanying these animal sacrifices, the true contrition experienced by the husband, the thanks of the couple for blessings received, and their legitimate prayers for the health and welfare of their whole family. In this imaginative exercise Sanders brings home how ordinary human needs can be served by this system or ecology of worship and morality.

Unlike many Ancient Near Eastern religious systems, which had secret rituals and spells known and performed by the priests alone, Judaism provided full explanations to everyone of each step in the ceremonies, with most of the sacrifices taking place at the public altar. While we may assume that there was music and singing at many ceremonies, the sacrifices themselves were conducted in silence. This may have been a deliberate stance or style to emphasize that magic spells were not being used. Even Moses prayed in private during some of the confrontation stories with the Pharaoh in Exodus. Milgrom suggests that this was a deliberate point in the traditions, so that Moses did not present himself to the Pharaoh as a caster of spells or a worker of mysterious religious arts. In general in Leviticus the priests worked with the laypeople during many parts of the rituals, as well as in their roles of teaching and judging, and it is best to consider these interrelations and acts of worship as a "partnership of trust" (Milgrom's term) between the priests and the people.

Before going on to the first chapter, I would like to include two lists from Milgrom showing possible layers of editing within Lev 1–16. The first list includes later expansions by P editors themselves (P2), and the second list shows some of the later editing by H editors. We will return to some of these details as we study individual chapters, but I think it is helpful to include both lists here. Neither list is extensive.

General Introduction to Leviticus

Some of the additions are easy to spot. The very first P2 insert, 1:14–17, adds a provision for using turtledoves or pigeons rather than herd animals, while the first H insert, 3:16–17, is an attempt to limit the slaughtering of animals for major family meals to shrine sites.

P2 Expansions in Lev 1–16	
1:14–17	Offerings of birds
2:3, 10, 14–16	Details about grain offerings
7:8–10	Priests' shares of certain offerings
8:3–5, 10–11, 26	Minor ceremonial items
9:21	Ceremonial detail
10:15	Priests' share of certain offerings
11:24–38, 47	Details on unclean foods or vessels
13:47–59	Details on unclean fabrics
15:33	Additional details about discharges
16:1	Historical connection to deaths of Aaron's two sons

H Editing in Lev 1–16	
3:16–17	Meat should be slaughtered at a shrine
6:19–23	Grain offering by priests
7:22–29, 38(?)	Details about fat and blood portions of offerings
9:17	Details about grain offerings
11:43–45	Details about swarming creatures and insects
12:8	Lesser offerings by the poor
14:34–57(?)	Details about molds in walls of houses
15:31	Reference to effects of uncleanness
16:2, 29–34	Additional rules for Yom Kippur

Milgrom reminds us that in Leviticus the focus on the fine details of rituals presupposes a common theological understanding shared by all the original readers. We will not need to note minor differences between P and H editorializing, except in a few cases. We can assume that the Holiness school built upon the beliefs and doctrines already found in Priestly traditions.

Our goal here is to acquire some of the theological understanding of our ancestors in the faith who were guided by the details in Leviticus. The reason for this is simply that we (Jews and Christians) worship the same Creator, even though those early rites have been permanently discontinued by the travails of Near Eastern history and replaced by consensus with alternative forms of prayer and worship.

Instructions for Study Groups

1. This book is designed for individuals or study groups more than for students in a traditional classroom. Students in class can rely on the teacher for explanations, assignments, and instructions. Individuals or groups have to shepherd themselves along. Groups have to decide many practical details—when, where, and how often to meet, and which members can lead in prayer, in providing refreshments, and in keeping the meeting place free of distractions. Experience suggests that groups should have about eight members. They should be willing to read some texts aloud, pray in common, and suggest ways to apply Scripture to daily life.

2. A group leader will have to read far enough ahead in this study guide to estimate how many biblical chapters can best be covered during each meeting. The leader should not tip off everyone about the answers beforehand.

3. The Answers section in this book should be examined for the first time at the group meeting, after everyone has shared their own answers (the leader holding back till last). Those who tend to be shy about speaking should be given a second personal invitation to participate before the group moves on. Should some answers or lines of analysis seem unsettling or untraditional, it may be best to revisit these at the start of the next session, after everyone has had time to think them over.

4. It will be easier for individuals or for groups to use one clear, academic biblical translation, such as the New Revised Standard Version (NRSV). The NRSV is used in this study guide except where I mention other translations or provide one of my own for a specific verse or phrase. Some English versions of the Bible

intended for a wider audience contain too many paraphrases to be useful in this task.

Leviticus 1:1—10:20

Section One

LEVITICUS 1:1—17

The first verse of the book shows God speaking to Moses from the tent of meeting. Moses is outside the tent, listening to the instructions. There are several ways to depict the dialogs between God and Moses. In some cases Moses is within the fore room of the tent while God is within the inner room, the holy of holies (see Exod 25:22; 30:6, 36; Num 7:89). When Moses is with the people, God's glory can fill the fore room also (see Exod 29:42-43; Lev 9:4-5, 23-24; Num 14:10; 16:19, 43; 20:6).

The intimate contact between God and Moses in Exod 24:15—25:1 can be contrasted with the more restricted communications in Exod 40:34-38 and Lev 1:1. The conferences about plans for the tabernacle are unique, but the instructions in Leviticus are of a lesser magnitude.

The Priestly writers usually avoid phrases that have Moses seeing God directly. The dramatic phrases in Exod 33:11; Deut 34:10; and Num 12:8 about seeing God *face to face* (in Num 12:8 *mouth to mouth*) are not from the Priestly traditions. Milgrom suggests we take them simply as ways of speaking of God's presence, rather than literal descriptions of what Moses himself experienced. Perhaps the Priestly editors were wary of leaving the impression that Moses had or should become an immortal or semi-divine figure.

Many scholars take the description of the cloud of glory that leads the people when they journey (Exod 40:36-38) as an interpolated text, which points toward the culmination of the ordination of Aaron and his sons in Lev 9:15-24. These two passages then serve to bracket all of Lev 1:1—9:14.

The reference to *any of you* (*adm*) in Lev 1:2 seems to refer to the people of Israel. Milgrom suggests that the instructions may have originally included resident aliens. They are mentioned in 22:18–25 in connection with other ceremonies, and in 24:17–21 in connection with blasphemy and other crimes.

In Hebrew the verb for *offer* or *sacrifice* (*qrb*) means to *bring something near* (*forward*), and the sacrifice itself is called *qorban, that which is brought near*. The word for *burnt offering* (*ola*) may come from a verb meaning to *rise* or *ascend*, perhaps referring to the extensive smoke from the total incineration. In the Pentateuch *burnt offerings* are usually mentioned first when discussing several ceremonies. Male animals were the most expendable, given that in herd management only a certain percentage of males were kept for breeding. The entrance of the tent of meeting includes what we would call the outer courtyard of the entire tabernacle. Lay people were not simply spectators; they brought the animals, laid their hands on the heads of the animals, slaughtered, flayed and quartered them, and presented the sacrifice to the priests. Those bringing the offerings were responsible to be sure they were unblemished; the priests also inspected the animals for the same reason.

Milgrom argues that when the donor puts a hand on the head of the animal it is simply a gesture of ownership. The donor of birds or offerings of flour or bread or monies does not perform the same gesture, because he or she is already carrying those offerings by hand—the normal gesture for someone who owns such goods. When indicating ownership by the placing of the hand, the donor would also tell the priest what type of sacrifice was intended. Some of the same animals could be used for offerings of well-being, as we will see in Lev 3.

In 1:5 the one who actually slaughters the animal is not identified; the Hebrew simply says that *one will kill it*. At times in English translations such phrases are put in a passive form (*the bull shall be slaughtered*), which also does not identify the subject. Context indicates that the person bringing the animal does the slaughtering, and the flaying, quartering, and cleaning mentioned in 1:6–9.

Ancient rabbinical commentary indicates that the custom was to point the animal's face toward the sanctuary at the moment of slaughter. Pagan custom often called for pointing the animal's head down at the ground; this is consistent with animism or ancestor worship. Other cultures had the head pointed up to the sky, the realm of the gods. In 1

Sam 14:32 Saul's soldiers slaughtered some cattle and sheep *on the ground* (*arzah*). The Hebrew could well mean *toward the ground*, i.e., having the animals' heads pointed down. At that point Saul had them use a stone altar, and gave stricter instructions about disposing of the blood of the animals before eating them. The mention that the soldiers sinned by eating meat with blood in it (1 Sam 14:33–34) might also have included the improper pointing of the animals' heads as well.

In Lev 1:5 the priests put the blood against the sides of the altar; blood was not put on top of the altar or incinerated in quantity with the sacrifices. Later, in the temple, there were special drains encircling the base of the altar, leading to an area for evaporation and proper disposition.

The donor then skinned the animal after severing the head and lower shins, quartered it as directed, and washed the entrails and leg areas to remove dung. The priests put new firewood on the glowing coals on the altar and then completely burnt the quartered pieces, head, and sections of suet, following the customary practice.

From other sources (Neh 10:35; 13:31 and rabbinical traditions) we learn that at the temple firewood was donated in quantity by leading families or tribes. The individual offerer would have been hard put to bring firewood at the time of the ceremony.

Milgrom modifies the traditional translation of *offering by fire* (*ishh*) in 1:9, 13, 17 to *food gift*. He derives this from non-Hebrew semitic root words for *gift*, and theorizes that it was an obsolete term even in pre-exilic times. Milgrom also notes that speaking of the *pleasing odor* (*reah nihoah*) of the sacrifices is another ancient phrase that became so standard as to lose much of its meaning. He cautions against using more melodramatic English words such as *appeasing, placating,* or *soothing,* since they can introduce many misimpressions about God.

Apparently bulls could be slaughtered anywhere near the altar (most likely on the east side, closer to the entrance into the outer courtyard) but sheep were to be slain at the north side (Lev 1:11). This may be due to practicalities; perhaps bulls were harder to shove around or the north side had fewer obstructions than the west or south, etc. In later temple structures there was a shambles, a series of hitching posts on the north side, making it easier to restrain any animal in that setting, so all animals were slaughtered there.

Milgrom suggests that 1:14–17 (on birds) was added later. Birds are not mentioned in 1:2, and the *If* at the start of 1:14 often indicates an entirely new topic. Further, the introduction in 1:2–3 gets picked up in 3:1, where no birds are mentioned at all.

Commentators take the birds as the honorable alternative for poor people. Turtledoves and pigeons were easily domesticated in ancient times. There was no need to limit to males, or to worry excessively about finding blemishes; they were so inexpensive no one would have gained by trying to palm off damaged birds to start with. Nor was there need to place a hand to show ownership. Priests were skilled at manually removing the head and all inner organs and the entire digestive tract (including the anus and tail with its feathers) within just a few seconds (using no other implements). All these, head and organs, were discarded at the ash pit and removed or reduced later, apart from the ceremony (1:16), since there was no point to washing or burning such small organs. Finally, the priest would crack the rib cage by hand to spread the wings further apart (perhaps just to make the shape larger or to have it burn more easily) and burn the gutted bird, feathers and all. The few drops of blood were sprinkled at the side of the altar.

Questions

1. Look at the basic instructions for a whole burnt offering in 1:3–9. How can such a complex holocaust be understood as an act of worship?
2. The instructions in 1:3–13 include the offerers and the priests. Who serves whom in all this?

Conclusion

Milgrom notes that *ola* can mean *burnt*. In context it might also have meant *entire* or *whole*; in Lev 6:23 a *whole offering* is a *kalil*, often an adjective but here a noun (see also Deut 33:10 and 1 Sam 7:9; in these cases the skin might have been left on the animal). Milgrom thinks that the *kalil* sacrifice was eventually replaced by the designation *ola* because a new tradition developed that the skin was to be removed and given to the priest, and so technically the sacrifice wasn't *whole* anymore. Milgrom prefers to call the *ola* a *burnt offering* in most instances.

Another question is whether *olas* were propitiatory or expiatory for individuals (as in Lev 1:4, the only P reference in Lev which speaks of this sacrifice as an *atonement*). Or did they rather serve as sacrifices for joyous adoration, vow fulfillment, or other freewill instances? In H sections (Lev 22:17–19; Num 15:3) only joyous adoration is stressed.

Milgrom finds many examples of all these motives, and suggests that originally *olas* were the only form of sacrifice needed beside *shelamim* (*peace offerings* or *offerings of well-being* that the people themselves ate). Later on in a larger temple more specific purification and reparation sacrifices could have been devised, so then the *burnt offering* would no longer need have been expiatory for any individual. Milgrom also notes that the public expiatory *olas* and later purification and reparation offerings were always of male animals, while in Lev 4:27–35; 14:10; Num 6:14, etc. a layperson was to bring a female animal for his individual purification rites. This could also indicate that the *ola* was the oldest form of sacrifice, originally using the expendable males.

Section Two

LEVITICUS 2:1–16

This chapter outlines various voluntary grain offerings. They are understood to be even less expensive substitutes in place of turtledoves or pigeons. Anyone (*nefesh*), man or woman, could bring these grain offerings.

Priestly writers consistently refer to such offerings as *gifts* (*minha*). The *choice flour* (*solet*) is semolina wheat, the larger inner kernels (grains or grits) that could be sifted from the smaller ground particles.

Quantities of flour or oil are not specified here. Olive oil could be poured on top of the flour or more thoroughly mixed with it. The oil would help the portion of flour or dough set aside to burn better, and was also used in ordinary dough anyway. Oil was a symbol of joy and health, but was never offered by itself.

Frankincense is mentioned in 2:3, 14–16; scholars consider it an optional enhancement that many poor people would not have used. A grain of this expensive resin, when used, could have been placed in plain sight near the edge of the mixture of flour and oil. Then the priest could take that bit to put in the fire, while saving the rest, as indicated. The rest of the flour and oil was given to all the priests, perhaps after being collected and remixed to a consistent texture.

In addition to flour mixed with oil, 2:4–10 allows worshippers to prepare baked or fried cakes or scones instead, made without yeast or incense. Token fragments (*azcrh*, perhaps from the verb *zcr*, to *remember* or *mention*) of these prepared cakes were burnt, and the rest was given to the priests. When the priests burned the bits of frankincense, of uncooked dough or of fully prepared cakes or scones, they were dedicating the entire gift to God. It was God's instruction to regift most of it to feed the priests and their families.

Milgrom suggests that while remixed quantities of flour and oil might have easily been shared by all the priests, it is likely that a single cake or wafer could more easily have been kept by just the one priest who presided. In 7:9–10 these customs seem to be in place. A somewhat similar division occurs in 7:31–33, where the right breast of an animal used in a sacrifice of well-being is reserved for all the priests, while the right thigh is given to the one priest involved in the ceremony. Milgrom argues that as time went on older shrine customs about what to share with the one priest there were merged with the sharing customs needed at the temple, with its much larger number of priests and dependents. Thus 2:3, 10 are likely to be glosses representing this later sharing with all the priests.

In 2:11 yeast and honey, leavening agents, may not be used in any offering that will be burnt on the altar. Milgrom proposes that the *honey* (*dbsh*) is fruit syrup, rather than honey from beehives. Lev 2:12 does allow for leavened bread to be brought for other ceremonies where nothing of it is burnt in sacrifice. In the ancient world the use of leavening agents was understood as an integral part of the process of making dough rise or grape juice turn into wine, but at least in Jewish thinking about clean and unclean foods these agents in themselves were taken as symbols of deterioration and death. Wine offerings were allowed at rituals, since these were poured at the base of the altar and never mixed with what was being burnt.

The final three verses (2:14–16) speak of *kernels* or *ears* (*abib*) of *coarse new grain* (*geresh*) offered at a first fruits ceremony. These are fresh kernels of barley, still soft and green. The Hebrew calls them *geresh carmel* (*grains from rich gardens*, whence the name *Mt. Carmel*).

Milgrom notes that Lev 2:14–16 is an appendix, which may refer to an obligatory presentation of first fruits by the community. Similar offerings mentioned in Num 18:13 and Neh 10:36 were obligatory. In Num 28–29, the great review of the liturgical calendar, the full ceremony is outlined in 28:26–31, where it seems that the grain was burnt along with other sacrifices. In Lev 23:9–14 the offering of first fruits may originally have been an obligation for individual farmers rather than the community as a whole. Milgrom takes Lev 23 to be from the Holiness editors, and notes that they are relying on Lev 2 and Num 28, earlier Priestly sources.

Question

3. In 2:1–10 offerings of flour and bread are described. How are they related to the offerings of Lev 1?

Conclusion

The noun *minha* (*gift*), which P uses for all these offerings of grain, has a wide range of meanings in the Old Testament. It can be a present made to gain or maintain respect or allegiance, or serve as an expression of thanks. Jacob gave such presents to Esau at a time when Jacob feared for himself and for his family (Gen 32:14–21; 33:10). Such presents often included animals, not just grain. In Gen 4:3–4 Cain gave God a *gift* of some of his crops and Abel gave a *gift* of some of the lambs of his flock. The NRSV calls them *offerings*, but both verses use *minha*.

Milgrom suggests that the many instances of flour used in ceremonies in the Pentateuch and elsewhere may indicate that these grain offerings were of ancient origin, and they may have in the past been offered in their own right instead of being thought of as substitutes for other offerings of animals or birds. In support of this suggestion Milgrom lists several instances in Leviticus and Numbers where flour and bread are used at various ceremonies.

Lev 6:19–23	Grain offerings by priests themselves
Lev 7:12–14	Thanksgiving sacrifices of well-being
Lev 8:26–28	Ordination ceremony
Lev 23:9–14	First fruits grain offerings
Lev 23:15–20	Offerings at festival of weeks
Lev 24:5–9	Twelve presentation loaves each Sabbath
Num 5:15, 25–26	Grain used in adultery trial by ordeal
Num 6:19–20	Bread used at Nazirite ceremony

In Jer 7:17–18 the prophet condemns his people for baking cakes to worship the queen of heaven and pouring libations to other gods. The topic comes up again in Jer 44:15–19, 24–26. In Jer 19:13 the prophet speaks of such offerings and libations being made on the rooftops of people's homes. Milgrom suggests that such abuses may have led the priests to confine grain sacrifices to the temple, and to have the flour and bread designated for the priests alone.

Section Three

LEVITICUS 3:1–17

The structure of Lev 3:1 is similar to that of 1:3, but now we find another voluntary type of sacrifice, one of well-being (*zeba shelamim*). The offerer may bring a male or female animal, since most of the meat will be taken away by the family. As with paschal lambs, the skin was also retained by the one making the offering.

Those segments of the animal set aside for burning include two large portions of suet protecting the entrails, namely the caul or greater omentum and the mesentery. These two slabs could be removed easily by hand. In addition the priests took the kidneys, the organs most entwined with fat. Another portion for burning was a particular appendage to the liver, the caudate lobe (which had to be cut with a knife). Milgrom suggests that the cutting of this lobe would have rendered the entire liver unfit for use in auguries, a common superstitious practice in the ancient world.

Lev 3:9 mentions the broad tails of sheep as another element for the burning. Some Near Eastern breeds of sheep have enlarged tails, much of which is fatty. With the exception of the kidneys themselves, all of the suet is inedible. Milgrom suggests that this large amount of suet would burn slowly and produce a lot of smoke. Perhaps the smoke itself would add to the solemn image of transforming the offering to the spiritual realm.

Lev 3:5 mentions the *burnt offering* (*ola*) already on the fire. Apparently this refers to the daily morning offering of a year-old male lamb (Exod 29:38–39; Num 28:3–4).

The very end of Lev 3:16 and all of 3:17 makes a broad statement that all offerings of suet belong to God. This may be a modification that came from Holiness editors. Milgrom assumes that this means that all ordinary slaughtering of cattle, sheep, and goats was required to take place at shrines. In other words, every major family celebration should involve a sacrifice of well-being at a shrine, even if that means that the celebration might have to be held near the shrine rather than at home. Fowl and game are not included in this broad statement. A somewhat parallel passage in Lev 7:22–27 may refer to animals not intended for sacrifice.

This association of well-being sacrifices with shrines was later modified in Deut 12:15–16, 20–24 since it would not have been practical for most people to hold such family celebrations in Jerusalem.

Question

4. How would you characterize the style of Lev 3? What is missing in this chapter?

Conclusion

The term *offering* or *sacrifice of well-being* (*zebah shelamim*) is an inclusive compound form that can include *thanksgiving offerings* (*zebah toda*), as in Lev 22:29; Pss 107:22; 116:17. We find *annual offerings* (1 Sam 1:21), *clan offerings* (1 Sam 20:29), *paschal offerings*, etc. In a general statement in Jer 7:21 *offerings* (*zebahim*) are eaten. All these are slain offerings, eaten by the worshipper and his family on joyous occasions. Milgrom suggests that some *thanksgiving offerings* were thought of as semi-obligatory and may have helped expand the use of sacrifices of *well-being* over time.

Milgrom notes that Lev 7:19–21 serves as a reminder that those partaking of a feast of well-being must be ritually clean themselves. In 1 Sam 2:12–14 the sons of Eli, priests at Shiloh, are depicted as taking too much meat too soon from sacrifices being offered and shared (some of the meat was being boiled in kettles). Some specific regulations, such as that the meat of these sacrifices must be consumed within one or two days at the most, may have stemmed from a shrine's own purity regulations.

There are many biblical citations, including Lev 9:4, 18; 23:19; Num 10:10, that speak of single well-being offerings representing the worship of the entire community. These might have developed from the individual sacrifices we have been examining. In some of these cases the priests (or other leaders) ate the food.

In Lev 8:31–32 and Exod 29:33–34 we may have the precedent for all sacrifices of well-being. In these passages Aaron and his sons share the meat of rams offered at their ordination ceremony. In Exod 29:27–28 the designation of one thigh and one breast for the priests echoes the extensive regulations about sharing some of the meat of well-being offerings that we will study in Lev 7:31–32. That chapter goes into much greater detail than what we find in Lev 3.

Section Four

LEVITICUS 4:1–35

Questions

To vary the format a bit, in the next two sections and at many points later on I will put the questions at the front of a section. This will give the reader a chance to get a feel for how much the original writers and editors felt free to condense or omit details, given that their fellow believers were aware of most of the current ceremonial customs.

5. In 4:3–12 the high priest is given directions for the blood of a bull used in a purification offering. In addition he is to burn the portions of suet and organs as at a sacrifice of well-being, and then have the rest of the bull incinerated at a clean place outside the camp. Suggest reasons for all these steps.

6. In 4:13–21 a similar offering is made for all of the people. What is different in this ceremony in comparison with the first?

7. In 4:22–26 a simpler ritual is outlined for an unintentional sin by a ruler (prince, chief). In what ways is it simpler?

8. In 4:27–35 a purification ritual is outlined for any ordinary Israelite. In what ways is it simpler than the previous three cases?

9. Assuming that we could come up with examples of unintentional sins by these parties, and that we could understand the sacrifices serving as sacraments of atonement, what is the main theological concern or viewpoint of the authors of this entire chapter?

While a newcomer to Leviticus might develop some feel for the spiritual logic of adoration in voluntary whole-burnt and well-being sacrifices, and for the use of birds or grain offerings for those who cannot afford larger whole-burnt offerings, the subject matter of Lev 4 is nearly incomprehensible at first. There is little explanation as to how anyone can sin *unintentionally*, and the details of the sacrifices vary considerably case by case. The only structure that is easily followed is the subdivision by sinning parties. So we speak of the anointed priest (the high priest) in 4:3-12, the entire nation in 4:13-21, an individual ruler (prince) in 4:22-26, and any individual Israelite in 4:27-35.

The word for *unintentional* in this chapter is the noun *shggh*, used with a preposition to mean *in ignorance* or *in inadvertence*. A reference to a sin committed in ignorance might be Job's remark in Job 6:24, *make me understand how I have gone wrong* (*shgg*). Inadvertent sins we have already studied would be the instances of accidental manslaughter explained in Num 35:22-23 and Deut 19:4-6.

Milgrom reminds us that Priestly editors always use the verb to *sin* (*hta*) to focus on how a sinful action offends God. Milgrom (229) describes this as an action that "sets up reverberations that upset the divine ecology. Specifically, in the Priestly conceptual scheme, an act forbidden by God generates impurity, which impinges upon God's sanctuary and land." In the worst case, if the sanctuary were to become extremely impure, God would abandon it altogether.

Milgrom notes that other ancient Near Eastern religions were concerned that rival gods or demons were always trying to attack sanctuaries, but in Jewish thinking it was the sins of people that posed the great, indeed the only, danger. Milgrom calls this a national dimension to ethics, and observes that ethical behavior is an indispensable factor in determining Israel's destiny. Passages such as Lev 26:14-39 draw a picture of God's aversion to sin in astounding degree. Milgrom refers to the Priestly editors as the precursors of the prophets in their concern for ethics.

The editors of Lev 4 speak of violations of *commandments about things not to be done*, but they provide no examples. Commentators suggest that many of these matters might be fine points of liturgical regulations, but Milgrom wants to include matters of ethics also. A high priest or a prince or an individual Israelite might admit in his heart that he did something unethical, even if no one else knew about such an inner failure. Many of the high priest's acts of worship were conducted within the tent, with no other witnesses. He would have to accuse himself of any inadvertent ceremonial lapses. The realization by any of these parties that some action was careless or unethical might have come sometime after the act itself.

Ancient rabbis suggested examples such as a high priest misidentifying a new moon by one day. Then the nation would be celebrating sacrifices on the wrong days for the rest of that month. Another example would be the wrong done by many people in following a false prophet for a time.

In Lev 4:3 the sin of the high priest, even if unintentional, *brings guilt on the people*. The Hebrew word for *guilt* (*ashmh*) can also mean *consequence of guilt*. The point is firmly made; the people will suffer or be punished for something the high priest did. In 10:6 Moses gives Aaron strict instructions following the divine punishment of two of Aaron's sons. He tells Aaron that if he disobeys in this case he *will die and wrath will strike all the congregation*.

In the NRSV of 4:13–14, 22–23, 27–28 the parties *incur guilt (ashm)*, but they learn of this in different ways. In 4:13 the matter had *escaped the notice* (*ylm*) of the assembly; later it *became known* or *was made known* (*idy*) to them. The same verb *idy* occurs in 4:23, 28. In these passages the verb *ashm* can mean not only *incurring guilt* but also *confessing* or *accepting the consequences* of that guilt (Milgrom translates that they *feel guilt*). So remorse and knowledge prepare one to bring a *sin offering* (*hattat*). Milgrom prefers to call these sin offerings *purification offerings*, for the sake of clarity. He notes that the noun *hattat* is based on the intensive form of the verb, and cites Num 19:19, where the ashes of the red heifer *purify* (*htta*) an unclean person at the end of the seven-day period. As we have noted, many neighboring ancient Near Eastern religions had purification rituals to decontaminate or protect their temples from hostile spiritual forces. I will follow Milgrom's lead from this point and use the term *purification offerings*.

The details of the *purification offerings* are quite varied, and no explanations are given for the differences. For the high priest or for the entire congregation a bull is sacrificed; a prince must offer a male goat; and an ordinary Israelite must bring a female goat or sheep. Milgrom suggests that a ruler might own large flocks of goats with males to spare, while a poorer farmer might have had just a few female goats or sheep with one or no males (paying stud fees as needed).

In the first two cases some of the blood from the bull is sprinkled by the high priest toward the curtain protecting the holy of holies, some is applied to the corners (horns) of the small incense altar in the outer room, and the rest is poured at the base of the main altar out in the open courtyard. For the prince or the ordinary Israelite some blood is applied to the corners (horns) of the main altar and the rest is poured around its base. These ceremonies can be performed by any priest. Milgrom argues that sprinkling and applying blood in this way consecrates it, thus making it an effective sacramental substance for the ceremonies. In ancient Near Eastern cultures purifying or protecting shrines and temples often involved applying significant substances to doorways, inner or outer corners of sacred rooms, or sharp edges and ledges of altars. Touching those areas effectively purified or protected the entire structure or altar.

In all four cases the special segments of fat, the kidneys, and the liver lobe are removed and burnt, as in offerings of well-being. Yet in the first two cases all the remaining parts of the bull are burnt in their entirety at a special place outside the camp. In the last two cases there is no mention of what happens to the remaining parts of the goats or sheep. Later in 6:24–30 we learn that the meat of these lesser *purification offerings* is to be consumed by the priests. There is no need to remove these animals to the special place outside the camp; they are handled at the main altar just as many other types of sacrifices. Milgrom theorizes that burning the bulls of purification for the high priest or for the nation in this manner could be understood as an extra precaution or dramatization of the seriousness of the original unintentional errors.

In summary statements in 4:33, 35 *purification offerings* are clearly distinguished from the whole-burnt and well-being offerings mentioned in chs. 1–3. Purification offerings are expiatory, but not gifts of adoration as such.

In Lev 4:20, 26, 31, 35 the text speaks of *atonement* and of God *forgiving* those involved. The verb to *forgive* (*slh*) always has God as subject and can mean to *have forbearance* or to *pardon*. Milgrom points to the instance in Num 14:19–23 where Moses begs God to *forgive* when the people and the scouts are afraid to fight the Canaanites. God says "I do *forgive*," but then he adds, "Nevertheless . . . none of the people who have seen my glory and the signs that I did in Egypt and in the wilderness, and yet have tested me these ten times and have not obeyed my voice, shall see the land that I swore to give to their ancestors; none of those who despised me shall see it."

This scene follows Num 14:18, with the famous quotation, "The LORD is slow to anger, and abounding in steadfast love, forgiving iniquity and transgressions, yet by no means clearing the guilty..." Different vocabulary is used here; God *takes away* (*nsa*) the iniquity, but he will not *declare to be exempt from punishment* (*nqh*). Yet *taking away* must mean something like *pardoning* or *forgiving*. In Exod 34:9 Moses asks God to *forgive* the unspeakably rebellious act of making the golden calf, and God immediately institutes the new covenant by decree (34:10).

Regarding the use of *slh* in Lev 4, Milgrom notes that these wrongs have dishonored the altar of God, and God's forgiveness restores the unity between himself and the individual or the whole people. In this context the word *forgive* is much richer than it might seem at first.

Conclusion

Milgrom mentions Num 15, a complex review of details at times of religious sacrifice. In Num 15:22–29 unintentional sins are treated, which now includes the mention of resident aliens (15:26, 29). Milgrom argues that this passage is based on independent traditions that might have developed later than those in Lev 4. In vivid terms Num 15:30–31 indicates that those who sin with a clear intention to do so are to be shunned by the community. Resident aliens are included in this condemnation.

Milgrom notes that in Num 19 the mixture of water and the red heifer's ashes, including the ashes of its blood, is used to purify people, not places of worship. The blood, even reduced to ash, is the purifying element. He theorizes that this is likely a remnant of ancient exorcism rituals that focused mainly on corpse contamination. A good example of an ancient exorcism might be found in Lev 14:1–9, 49–53. In these two cases priests sprinkle blood on a leper or on fungal growths on house walls. One bird is sacrificed for the blood and a second one is dipped in the blood and released unharmed to fly away. By contrast, in using the mixture of water and the ashes of the red heifer, any pure person can preside (Num 19:18, 19, 21), and there is no sending away of any other animal or bird. Milgrom argues that the Lev 14 rites are much older than the less dramatic use of the sacramental waters in Num 19.

Rituals have their own inner logic. Milgrom mentions one pagan custom of burying a special religious figurine after it was used to remove a curse from someone. The figurine was buried in a deep hole, and after the soil was packed down over it small nails were pounded into the soil to further "imprison" the figurine. This may sound silly to us, but the ceremony was a way of expressing that polytheism.

Milgrom also speculates that purification rituals grew more complex during the temple period, having had their start long before in the custom of whole-burnt offerings. We will not review these matters here.

I think it is more important for us to appreciate the idea of sins, even inadvertent ones, tainting the place of worship. Milgrom uses several analogies to prick our imaginations. He speaks of the power of sin as an *aerial miasma*, a *dynamic, implacable foe* of life, an invisible power such as *magnetism* or *electromagnetic charge*. He uses another analogy, that of *The Picture of Dorian Gray*. Here the inadvertent sinners seem to suffer no consequences, but God's view of the portrait of the temple is that it is being damaged and disgraced. The greater the sin, the more damage is done.

Similar analogies of invisible forces can help us to think of the holiness of the temple itself. I recall one commentator years ago developing the image of the temple as a nuclear power plant, with the priests acting as the nuclear safety engineers, keeping everything under control so that there would be no offense to cause a meltdown or explosion of God's wrath. A much more positive analogy by Walter Brueggemann describes coming to the temple as the opportunity to have a royal audience with the LORD, the king (650–79, esp. 656, 664). The point of all these images is that we have a corporate relationship with God, reaching back to Sinai. Beside the prayer of individuals, worship must also be communal. We pray together; we sin together; we seek forgiveness together.

Section Five

LEVITICUS 5:1–13

Questions

10. How does 5:1–6 differ from Lev 4?
11. How is 5:1–6 similar to Lev 4?
12. How do the last clause in 5:4, and all of 5:5 and 5:13, function within the entire passage of 5:1–13?

Ancient and modern students of Leviticus have all had trouble with the organization of topics in chs. 5–6. Following Milgrom's lead, we will take 5:1–13 to be an appendix containing modifications or expansions of Lev 4. In the Hebrew all the verses are in the third person; the NRSV changes everything to the second person. This minor change might help with clarity in English.

The chapter opens by profiling four specific sins: failing to come forward as a witness for a trial, touching unclean things (animal carcasses and the residue of human genital discharges are given as examples), or uttering a rash oath. Lev 5:1 simply notes that one failing to come forward as a witness shall bear his *punishment* (*ywn*). In small towns or villages a plaintiff or defendant in criminal or property cases could call upon potential witnesses (perhaps in the manner of a town crier), using an *adjuration* or *curse formula* (*alh*) to remind everyone of the seriousness of the obligation in justice to come forward. The reference to *punishment* (*ywn*) always means *punishment by God* in the Priestly texts.

Lev 5:2 explains that the touching of the carcass is *hidden* (*ylm*) from the person in question, but at some point that person is *guilty* or *feels guilt*; in 5:3–4 the touching of human discharges or the like is *hidden*, and then the person knows it and is *guilty* or *feels guilt*. The same is true for the one swearing *rashly* (*bta*). Rash oaths by men and women were mentioned in Num 30.

Milgrom notes that some of these wrongs, such as the failure to come forward as a witness and the rash manner of making an oath, cannot be considered unintentional. Yet they are now tied into the system of purification offerings explained in Lev 4. The word for *penalty* in 5:6–7, *asham*, can also mean *guilt offering* (as in 2 Kgs 12:16).

What links the four specific sins together? Milgrom argues that the link is the hiatus or the delay between the action and the sensing of guilt. The hiatus is vaguely described as a time when something *is hidden* but eventually *becomes known*. One could assume that the hiatus stems from accidental neglect or inadvertence, but the sanctuary is contaminated nonetheless, and over time this will get worse.

It might help to think of someone knowing that he or she should not handle a certain animal carcass or objects stained from discharges, but that if such contact were necessary simple purification customs should take place as soon as possible. If the person in question puts this obligation of purification "on the back burner," it might well stay there for weeks or months despite good intentions. Most of us do the same.

Milgrom also suggests that perhaps an old law with an absolute obligation to be a witness has here been modified to deal with someone who left that obligation on the back burner but later feels guilty and wants to confess his failure. The *punishment* mentioned is now simply to bring the *purification offering* described in this chapter.

The rash oath of 5:4 was most likely a promise to do something for God, but the promise was then put on another one of those back burners in our lives. Oaths were never obligatory, but once taken they involved God's honor. Failure to perform them completely and in a timely fashion was taken as a very serious matter, something that also contaminated the sanctuary. The phrase *for a bad or good purpose* is an idiom meaning *for any purpose* (see Gen 31:24; 2 Sam 14:17).

Lev 5:1, the matter of failing to be a witness, does not mention any hiatus or neglect, and does not speak of one *feeling guilt*. Milgrom (300–301) argues that, despite the lack of these phrases in 5:1, the broader statements in 5:4b–5 cover the entire opening paragraph. He translates 5:4b–5 as "and, though he has known it, the fact escapes him but (thereafter) he feels guilt in any of these matters. ⁵ When he feels guilt in any of these matters, he shall confess that wherein he did wrong." The NRSV has substantially the same effect, with "when you come to know it, you shall in any of these be guilty. ⁵ When you realize your guilt in any of these, you shall confess the sin that you have committed." Confessing this guilt was to be done in public, mentioning God or an injured human party or both, depending on the case. By adding the requirement of *confession* (an intensive form of a Hebrew verb meaning to *praise* [*ydh*]), Priestly traditions mitigated or reassigned these misdemeanors to the level of unintentional or inadvertent sins.

Milgrom finds this topic of confession to be of major import. He remarks that here repentance reduces the penalty for sin, without doing away with the penalty altogether. Here people are reassured that confession and repentance are desired by God; later on prophets will describe these motions of the heart in greater detail.

In 5:7 one bird serves for a purification offering and the other for a whole-burnt offering. Milgrom notes that some of the meat from the purification offering is reserved for the priest (as in 6:26). Since a bird is so small, a second one was used in a whole-burnt sacrifice to augment the ceremony, since they were meant as a substitute offering in place of a sheep or goat.

We have noted how Lev 5:4b–5 envelopes everything in 5:1–4. By the same token 5:13 speaks of *whichever of these sins one has committed*, thus connecting all of 5:6–13 with 5:4b-5.

Section Six

LEVITICUS 5:14—6:7

Note: The Hebrew numbering has twenty-six verses in Lev 5 and twenty-three in Lev 6. The English system has only nineteen verses in Lev 5 but thirty in Lev 6. Both systems agree again at the start of Lev 7. I will use the English numbering system throughout.

The next thirteen verses also cover both inadvertent and deliberate sins, and we need to consider what these specific cases have in common. Lev 5:14 speaks of *trespassing* (*myl*) *unintentionally* (*sggh*) and *sinning against* any of *the holy things of the LORD*. The verb *myl* is often translated as *being unfaithful*. It is used in Num 5:12 of the wife suspected of adultery. *Being unfaithful* or *trespassing* against holy things can also be called *committing a sacrilege*. The party guilty of the sacrilege must make *restitution* (the verb is from *shalom*, the word for *peace* or *prosperity*), and add a 20 percent penalty, all payable to the priests. Then the guilty one brings a ram to the altar for a *guilt offering* (*ashm*). Commentators assume that a priest assesses the cost of the sacrilege and of the animal.

This guilt offering is clearly akin to the *purification* or *sin* offerings mentioned earlier. Milgrom, after a thorough study of Hebrew vocabulary, prefers to call the guilt offerings *reparation offerings*, given the contexts. I will use his term. An unusual provision in this ritual is that the *monetary equivalent* of the ram may be used instead. The verb in Lev 5:15, 18; 6:6 is *yrk*, to *estimate a value*. In an older text, 2 Kgs 12:16, *money* from guilt offerings and sin offerings is mentioned. In 1 Sam 6 there is a long story about gold figurines donated as a guilt offering when the Philistines returned the ark of the covenant.

What these verses in Lev 5 do not provide is any detail as to what holy things have been dishonored or what precise sacrilege has taken place.

Milgrom notes that the topic in 5:17–19 was a great worry in ancient Near Eastern cultures. The fear of possibly having committed an unknown sacrilege could lead to psychic and physical stress. The offering of a ram as a reparation offering might help to allay those fears. If unexplainable suffering was thought to be a result of sin, one would search for that sin. Wrongdoing creates guilt and fear of punishment, and suffering reinforces the presence of guilt feelings because it is interpreted as punishment for sin.

Milgrom argues that the notion of sacrilege is being used in its widest range; it covers unintentional or deliberate dishonoring of whatever belongs to God, and will also be extended to various examples of cheating one's neighbor in 6:1–6. The wide range can cover all present and future cases.

Milgrom mentions one interesting pagan example of traditional sacrileges connected with rituals: the ancient Hittite text known as *Instructions for Temple Personnel*. The various warnings in this decree to priests, acolytes, and shrine workers about pilfering offerings and supplies or making shoddy substitutions for them remind one of the inside opportunities that employees have in large department stores. They often contribute to shoplifting losses much more than do the customers.

Lev 5:17–19 echoes somewhat the unintentional sins of the earlier sections of Lev 4. Here a person has *unknowingly committed an unknown sin* (*shgg shggh*) against any of the LORD's commandments, and *did not know it* (*lo-idy*), yet he has *sinned* and bears his *guilt* (*ywn*). As in 5:1 the guilt or *punishment* (*ywn*) will have to come from God alone. Milgrom notes that the phrase *without knowing it* may be more forceful than the phrases in those cases outlined in Lev 4. Milgrom suggests that perhaps 5:17 was once an independent law, now linked to 5:18–19, and the three verses are linked to 5:14–16 by placement.

The topic changes again in 6:1–7. Now *being unfaithful to the LORD* means *deceiving* (*chsh*) or *defrauding* (same verb) a neighbor in matters of deposit, pledge, robbery, or keeping a found item. Lev 6:3, 5 mention *swearing falsely* (*shby-al-shqr*) in any of these cases. Of course, any false oath *desecrates* (*hll*) God's name (see 19:11–12). Apparently in the average case the plaintiff might not have much leverage. If there were no other witnesses to the agreement of deposit or pledge, or to the true ownership of the found or stolen object, the defendant could simply make a false oath and likely succeed.

So restitution plus 20 percent is made to the injured party rather than to the priest, before the reparation ceremony is undertaken. Confession is implicit in Lev 4, and clearly mentioned in Lev 5:5 and Num 5:7 (*ydh*, form of verb to *praise*). Milgrom finds these two passages, Lev 6:1–7 and Num 5:5–9, to be the foundation stories for this way of converting deliberate sins to more easily forgivable ones as we have seen. He considers this process of converting to be a pre-exilic Priestly innovation, developed more fully later by the prophets.

Milgrom lists Lev 5:1–4; 6:1–7; 16:21 (confessing over the scapegoat) as the only cases in all of P where confession and sacrifice combine to bring about expiation. He even compares this process to the twelve steps of AA (Alcoholics Anonymous), which elicit remorse, confession, and restitution when possible.

Questions

13. Milgrom argues that in many verses in Lev 5–6 the verb *asham* should be translated *he (or you) feels guilt*. The NRSV translations are listed here:

Lev 5:2	*you are guilty*
Lev 5:3	*you shall be guilty*
Lev 5:4	*you shall be guilty*
Lev 5:5	*you realize your guilt*
Lev 5:17	*you have incurred guilt*
Lev 6:4	*you realize your guilt*
Lev 6:5	*when you realize your guilt* (Hebrew infinitive form)
Lev 6:7	*you incur guilt* (same infinitive form)
Num 5:6	*that person incurs guilt*

What could be gained by using the phrase *feeling guilt* in these verses?

14. Compare the style of Lev 6:1–7 with the similar passage in Num 5:5–8.
15. Compare Lev 6:1–7 with 5:1–6 for content.
16. We have mentioned the importance of publicly confessing the sins in 5:1–6; 6:1–7; 16:21. How does this help the sinner? How does it help someone in a twelve-step program?

Conclusion

Milgrom points to the benefits, for anyone feeling guilt for one of these serious events, of taking the initiative to offer a reparation sacrifice. The spirit of repentance is what makes the difference. The writers are not trying to create a scrupulous mindset in the readers; they are trying to show that restitution and repentance can lead to a new sense of purity and a restored relationship with God.

Section Seven

Leviticus 6:8—7:38

The next section contains regulations explaining or adding new details about some of the previous rituals. A rough outline might be helpful. Verses marked with the letter H may be later Priestly additions in the Holiness style, which we will find in the latter half of the book of Leviticus. Lev 7:22–27 is in the second-person plural, and a style change not noticeable in English.

Verses	Topic	Related to
Lev 6:8–13	whole-burnt offerings	Lev 1:3–17
Lev 6:14–18	cereal/grain portions	Lev 2:1–3
Lev 6:19–23 (H)	high priest cereal offering	Exod 29:39–41
Lev 6:24–25a (H)	"	"
Lev 6:25b–30	purification portions	Lev 4:1–5:13
Lev 7:1–7	reparation offerings	Lev 5:14–26
Lev 7:8–10 (H)	grain portions	Lev 2:2–7; 5:4–13; 6:25b–30
Lev 7:11–21	various well-being rules	Lev 3; 11; 27:9–13
Lev 7:22–27 (H)	fat and blood rules	Lev 1:5; 3
Lev 7:28–29a (H)	"	"
Lev 7:31–32	"	"
Lev 7:29b–36	well-being portions	Lev 2:2–3; 3
Lev 7:37–38	conclusion; 38b may be H	

While many of the rules are directed toward the priests, 7:11–36 is directed to lay people. Milgrom notes that the ancient rabbis saw the first five chapters of Leviticus as divided between voluntary (1–3) and mandatory sacrifices (4–5). By contrast, chs. 6–7 focus on the priestly role and support system. So 6:8—7:10 has to do with most holy sacrifices (note the term *most holy* in 2:3; 6:17, 25; 7:6), while 7:11–36 deals with more ordinary sacrifices. In some of these the priest takes his portion at the time of sacrifice (6:16; 26; 7:7–10), and in others the laity sets aside the priest's portion beforehand (7:32).

The Hebrew word for *ritual* in 6:9 is *torah*, perhaps better translated as *instruction* or *law*. The final burnt offering and the other collections of suet and organs of the day are to smolder on the coals of the altar all night (see Exod 29:38–41; Lev 1:10–13). The column of smoke would be visible to anyone within sight of the sanctuary, and could serve as a sign of the constant stance of adoration to which we are all called.

Linen vestments were used to minimize overheating and sweating. The priest responsible for removing ashes to the special clean location outside the camp had to change from his ritual linen vestments to appropriate secular clothing for this chore. The portion of grain or cereal offerings for the priests mentioned in Lev 6:14 adds information to the basic instructions of Lev 2.

Milgrom notes that the cereal offering in 6:20 probably refers to the daily offering of the high priest himself. The cost of the flour was borne by the sanctuary. Early rabbis were unsure if the offering was only for the day of ordination or if it applied only to Aaron's own immediate sons. Milgrom translates *on the day* in 6:20 as *from the time* to help clarify that this was to be a perpetual daily offering.

Lev 7:2–5 is the first detailed instruction regarding the sacrifice of the animal for a reparation offering. In 5:14—6:7 the focus was on monetary restitution. The disposition of the hide of the animal in 7:8 is new, as is the priestly portion of grain in 7:9–10. Apparently priests were to be given the hides of most animal sacrifices, except for the well-being category, in which case the hides were kept by the ones bringing the offering. In Jerusalem there were commercial tanneries to handle the trade.

In 7:9–10 note is made of grain portions for one priest and for the entire priesthood. This point of sharing is also brought up in 6:26, 29 and 7:33–34. Milgrom suggests that we might think of the way waiters and waitresses share tips as an analogy.

In 7:12 the *thanksgiving* offering is the original name for what P generally calls offerings of *well-being*.

In 7:14 the *gift* is a *teruma*; at one time older translations called this a *heave offering*. Milgrom explains that these gifts were designated by the offerer prior to any ritual, even before coming to the sanctuary. The word *teruma* is frequently used of donations of money or materials never used in rituals at all.

The giving of one thigh to the individual officiating priest in 7:28–36 is unlike the references in 9:21 and 10:15, where the thigh seems to be shared by all the priests. Milgrom suggests that the verses in chs. 9–10 are interpolations meant to overrule the passage in Lev 7. But since the passage in Lev 7 is not emended we are left with the two traditions in contradiction. This was a common editorial practice in ancient Israel—save everything, even if contradictions persist in the final larger text.

Milgrom takes Lev 7:35–36 to be a specific conclusion for 7:11–34. This is in line with the style found in Exod 29:27–28. Milgrom takes the next phrases in Lev 7:35–36a as a broader conclusion for all of 6:8—7:36. All of the laws came down from *Mount Sinai*.

Lev 7:38b, which mentions offerings brought in *the wilderness of Sinai*, could be an attempt to tie together all of chs. 1–7. Lev 6:8—7:36 is closely related to many points in chs. 1–5, as shown in the chart at the beginning of this section. The description in 7:38b hints at practices after the people left Mount Sinai and started their forty years of wandering.

The next chapter, Lev 8, picks up the story line from Exod 40, the point at which the tabernacle is completed. Exod 29 outlines the instructions for these ordinations, but they take place in Lev 8.

Question

17. Comment on the style and the general content of 6:8—7:38.

Conclusion

Milgrom argues that the broadest consensus in the logic of sacrifices is that they are gifts to induce divine aid—that God grant some blessing or protection, or accept atonement and contrition. In any sacrifice some piece of real property is transferred to divine purposes.

Other elements of faith are also present in any sacrificial system, and we cannot point to any one profile as entirely satisfactory for a single culture, nation, or region.

The *elevation offering (tenupa)* mentioned in 7:30, 34 was called a *wave offering* in older translations. It is always a liturgical action within the sanctuary. The owner of what is to be sacrificed must perform some kind of dedication ritual just before the sacrifice.

The burnt, cereal, purification, and reparation offerings do not have this term used with them since those materials were already dedicated before the ceremonies began. In fact the term *tenupa* is almost entirely limited to well-being offerings. Some other specialized or rare ceremonies included *tenupa*, apparently to provide additional assurances of sanctification. The verb behind the noun, *nwp*, can mean to *raise* (see Isa 10:15; 11:15; 13:2; 19:16). The *raising* serves as the sign of dedication. Milgrom takes this very simple gesture of dedication to be different from any more complex or continuous motion that we could call *waving*. He argues that those motions stem from ancient exorcism rituals and that the term *wave offering* should not be used to translate *tenupa*.

Another mistaken old term, *heave offering (teruma)*, occurs twice in Lev 7. The underlying verb, *rwm*, can mean to *raise* or *lift up*. In the NRSV of 7:14 it is translated as *gift* and in 7:32 it appears as *offering*. Milgrom uses the word *gift* in 7:32 for clarity. It seems to be an act of gifting done well prior to or outside of liturgical rites. In 7:32 the gift of the right thigh is given to the priest before the well-being ritual. The understanding of commentators is that the priest would only make use of this gift after the ceremony was complete. *Teruma* is also used at times to refer to a *tithe*. Ancient rabbis apparently took the complex description in Exod 29:26–27 as the basis for the motions of *waving* and *heaving* (*up and down*). The passage is:

> [26]... and you shall *elevate* [*nwp*] it as an *elevation offering* [*tenupa*] before the Lord.... [27] And you shall sanctify the breast of the *elevation offering* [*tenupa*] and the thigh of the *gift* [*teruma*] which is *elevated* [*nwp*] and *lifted up* [*rwm*] from the ram of consecration...

Section Eight

LEVITICUS 8:1–36

The next three chapters outline the ordination rites for Aaron and his sons, describe their first sacrifices for themselves and for all the people, and end with some rules and regulations and a stern account of the deaths of two of Aaron's sons. We will study each chapter individually.

Within the Pentateuch the original directions for the priestly vestments and the ordination ceremonies were given in Exod 28–29, and the tabernacle was constructed (but not consecrated) in Exod 35–40. We can take Lev 8:1–2 as the link to the earlier instructions in Exod 29. Milgrom proposes that Exod 39; 40:17–33 and Lev 8 may at one time have been consecutive texts, now separated by Exod 40:34–38 and Lev 1–7.

Milgrom notes that in Lev 1–7 Moses had to learn more details about various types of sacrifices before commissioning Aaron in his priestly role, and so the consecration of the tabernacle and of Aaron himself now occurs in Lev 8:10–12. This last passage seems to be later than those in Exod 29; 40 and Lev 16, which touch on the same topic. One could point to Exod 29:7 and 40:10 to see what the author of Leviticus was trying to link together.

So the preliminaries to the ceremony are mentioned in Lev 8:6–9, 12–13. The core of the rite is the three sacrifices: purification in 8:14–17, whole-burnt in 8:18–21, and ordination offering in 8:22–29. In 8:31–35 we find out that Aaron and his sons must stay within the tabernacle courtyard for seven full days before the ordination is finished.

There is an account of the dedication of the temple in the time of Solomon in 1 Kgs 8–9. Milgrom suggests that the references to the *whole congregation* in Lev 8:3–5 and to the consecration of the tabernacle and altar in Lev 8:10–11 might be borrowed from 1 Kings, thus making stronger theological links between the two dedications.

Milgrom is convinced of the fact that Lev 8:10–11 and 8:30 are interpolations. The reference to anointing the altar, the utensils, and Aaron now precedes the purification of the altar in 8:15, but the two stages should be reversed; purification should always precede consecration. So now in Leviticus we have Aaron consecrated long before his sons (8:30). In fact Aaron seems to be consecrated a second time in 8:30, which many commentators find unusual. In Exod 29:20–21 the various purifications and anointings seem to fit together more logically. Milgrom suggests that we must simply live with the differences between Exod 29 and Lev 8; the two traditions do not need to be reconciled.

In Lev 8:6–9 Aaron is fully vested as high priest before being anointed. Some of the vestment fabrics were identical to ones used in various tabernacle curtains. The *ephod* was similar to what we would call a full apron, with some provision to support the portion covering the chest.

Aaron's sons are vested in 8:13 in simpler fashion, but not anointed, although Aaron and his sons received a second sprinkling of oil and blood on their vestments in 8:30. Their sashes were something like Aaron's, and something like the outer curtain of the tabernacle. In that period wool was the only fiber easily dyed in bright colors.

Milgrom indicates that this late notice of the sons being vested, after having been washed earlier in 8:6, led ancient rabbis to changing the order of some of these verses, so that the sons would have been vested in a more timely fashion. I'm sure modern readers would not have paid much attention to the time gap between vv. 6 and 13.

The *Urim* and *Thummim* were apparently specially shaped stones or bones used to cast lots, to be used only by the high priest within the tabernacle. This custom of using lots eventually died out. Milgrom suggests that the custom may have been deliberately terminated by priests at some point because of its secular use by kings (1 Sam 10:22; 2 Sam 2:1; 5:23–24), or by lay people in superstitious or idolatrous ways (as hinted at in Hos 4:12; Hab 2:18–19; Zech 10:2).

In 8:15 the blood of the bull was used to *purify* (*hta*) the altar, perhaps from minor infractions by the candidates over the seven days they had to remain around the clock within the sanctuary (8:33). The mention of *atonement* in 8:15 may refer to the future role of the altar, rather than linking purification and atonement into one combined sacramental action. Usually purification and atonement were sought in separate rituals. Milgrom (524) paraphrases the verse by saying, "Thus he consecrated it *to effect atonement upon it.*"

In 8:17 some meat from this animal could have been given to Moses, but he was not considered a priest himself in P traditions. Another theory is that 8:17 preserves an older tradition in which all the meat of this sacrifice was burnt.

Likewise, in 8:29 Moses receives only the breast portion of the ram of ordination, where 7:31–36 indicates that he could have received more were he considered to be a priest himself. In a sense, Moses receives the priestly portion for his temporary role as master of ceremonies at a time when there were no priests yet ordained. In 8:27–28 it seems that Moses placed the thigh portion and some of the bread offerings on the hands of Aaron and his sons, and then removed the same objects and had them burnt. This might also be a way of indicating that the candidates for priesthood, although not yet fully ordained, had a more central role to play than Moses himself.

In 8:22 the ram of *ordination* (*mlaim*, from the verb *mla*, meaning to *fill* or *install*) is an offering ranked between more sacred sacrifices (such as whole-burnt, cereal, purification, etc.) and well-being or thanksgiving sacrifices. This intermediate type of sacrifice matches the situation, in which these ordinary Israelites are in transition between lay and priestly states. In 8:33 the root *mla* is used three times: "You shall not go outside . . . until the day when the period of your *ordination* is *completed*. For it will take seven days to *ordain* you."

In Lev 8:31–35 it might surprise readers to learn that Aaron and his sons must remain within the sanctuary for seven days. This could correspond to the mention of seven days in Exod 29:30–37. Apparently most of the ordination sacrifices were repeated each day, with the meat of each ordination ram and the bread offerings providing the food for Aaron and his sons.

The first part of Lev 8:36, mentioning the obedience of Aaron and his sons, may refer primarily to 8:31–35, the regulations for the seven days of confinement.

As in Exod 29:9, the original ordination ceremony does not have to be repeated for each generation; after this ceremony by Moses the priesthood simply became hereditary.

Questions

18. How do 8:12–13 and 8:30 assist us in reading this chapter?

19. The phrase *as the LORD commanded Moses* appears quite often in Lev 8, along with four other uses of the word *command*. Why do the editors place such a heavy emphasis on God's initiative?

20. How do Aaron and his sons participate in all the ceremonies in Lev 8? Are these events much different from the pattern of blessing or commissioning ministers that is fairly common in Christian denominations?

21. In the ceremonies in Lev 8, and for that matter in Lev 1–7 as well, there are no prayer formulas or texts, although we have minute details for everything else. Why were prayer texts not provided?

Conclusion

In the ancient Near East anointing was used in various legal and religious settings. Ancient Israelites normally used it only for religious meanings, eventually extending it to indicate God's blessings upon their kings. The image was also used metaphorically to indicate God's approval of patriarchs, prophets, or even of the Persian emperor Cyrus (Isa 45:1). Milgrom argues that as we read Lev 8 we should think mainly of the seven-day period of separation of Aaron and his sons from everyone else. That period is the heart of this ordination ceremony. The anointing simply set them apart from everyone else for this sacrament.

Section Nine

LEVITICUS 9:1–24

Immediately following the completion of their ordination, Aaron and his sons perform their first public sacrifices, some of which concern priests alone, while others are offered for all the people. Moses continues to guide and assist, but he does not co-officiate with the new priests in their specific roles. The appearance of the LORD in fire at the end of the chapter is a miraculous presence, even though Moses hints at it in 9:6. Milgrom calls this hint a "happy prognostication."

After opening preparations (9:1–7), Aaron offers a purification offering for himself (9:8–11), and also a whole-burnt offering (9:12–14). He then goes on to offer similar purification and whole-burnt offerings for the people (9:15–17). The mention of an offering of well-being (9:18–21) is unusual, because that was always a voluntary, indeed festive, form of worship. The editors assume that we understand how appropriate this well-being offering will be in this context.

The final scene involves blessings by Aaron, a brief move by Aaron and Moses to stand before the holy of holies within the tabernacle itself, followed by joint blessings of the people by both of them. God in his glory (in the form of fire) instantly reduced to ash all the sacrifices being burnt; this great sign was seen by all (9:22–24).

The details of the sacrifices focus mainly on what is put upon the altar; other customary instructions are omitted or abbreviated. The mention of a yearling calf and lamb for whole-burnt sacrifices (9:3) is another indicator of the festive nature of the day, perhaps developed from Num 28. The mention of *the LORD appearing* (9:4) is the only time in all the P traditions where the usual term *the glory (kabod) of the LORD* is not used (as in 9:6, 23). The *glory* is the combination of cloud and fire that masks the divine presence so as not to overwhelm human senses.

The appearance of God in this chapter will forever enhance the portable shrine, making it the equivalent of Mt. Sinai. In fact in P traditions the tabernacle and sanctuary may be even more important than the Sinai experience. At Sinai people heard God's voice from within the cloud and fire, but only select elders were able to come closer. Here everyone will see the bright flame of God's presence consume the sacrifices.

Moses instructs Aaron to *draw near (qrb) to the altar* (9:7). Various forms of this verb and noun are used ten times in this chapter. The NRSV uses *draw* or *drew near* in 9:5, 7, 8, *presented* in 9:9, 15, 16, *offering of the people* in 9:7, 15, *offer* in 9:2, and *entrails* in 9:14. In context the command of Moses in 9:7 for Aaron to *draw near to the altar* can certainly mean to *officiate*, to *begin his active role as main celebrant*. Ancient commentators even alluded to uses of this verb in romantic senses, and called Aaron's role an intimate act of adoration, the highest privilege God allows humans.

In 9:8 Milgrom prefers to translate that Aaron *came forward* to the altar, adding a bit to the sense that he will now *officiate*. In fact, his first task was to slaughter the calf for his purification offering, a task not performed close to the altar at all.

In 9:17 the mention of the *burnt offering of the morning* is likely an anachronism from later temple practice, although there are related references in Exod 29:38–40; 40:29 and Num 28:4–6. Likewise, the reference to the *right thigh* in Lev 9:21 may be out of place.

There is no reason given for the entry of Moses and Aaron into the tent of meeting itself. Milgrom suggests that they may have prayed for God to appear, assuming that Moses' earlier statement in 9:6 was a fond wish but not an ironclad guarantee. There is a good parallel in Solomon's inauguration of the temple. He blessed the people twice (1 Kgs 14–21, 54–61), and between the blessings prayed for forgiveness and protection for Israel (1 Kgs 14:22–53).

The *glory (kabod) of the LORD* then appeared to all, and the fire of the glory, without its usual cloud, consumed the sacrifices on the altar. There is a close parallel in 2 Chr 7:1–3, where fire from heaven struck the offerings made by Solomon at the dedication of the temple. At that point the glory of the LORD filled the temple, and everyone worshiped and gave thanks. Milgrom concludes that both appearances of consuming fire show divine favor. Aaron's priestly leadership is pleasing to God, as was Solomon's construction of the temple. In this tradition in Lev 9:24 the fire *came out from the LORD*. This could mean that it came roaring out from the holy of holies itself.

Question

22. How do you think the Israelites felt about their system of prayers and offerings by the end of Lev 9?

Conclusion

As Milgrom notes, the ark of the covenant was placed in the tabernacle (Exod 40:20–21) before the glory of the LORD descended upon it (Exod 40:34–35). So too, the ark was installed in Solomon's temple (1 Kgs 8:3–6) before the glory descended (1 Kgs 8:10–11). In these traditions God's presence is distinct from the ark itself. The latter is only a holy relic, and not a guarantee of God's favor. God can come and go as he sees fit.

Section Ten

LEVITICUS 10:1–20

At this point in the inaugural tabernacle ceremonies, readers could hardly expect the scenes that unfold in this chapter. In 10:1–7 Aaron's two oldest sons are consumed by divine wrath for using *unholy* or *unauthorized fire* in their censers. The Hebrew adjective, *zarah*, can mean anyone or anything *foreign*, *unlawful*, or *forbidden*. The *fire* must mean the glowing coals or embers put in the censer itself.

Further instructions about priestly duties and portions of food set aside for them and their families can be found in 10:8–15. This passage does not shed any light on the stunning event in 10:1–7.

Finally, in 10:16–20 Moses is very upset over the burning of the people's purification offering, some of the meat of which should have been consumed by the priests. Aaron defends his decision in this case to have the sacrifice burnt instead, and mentions *all that had befallen him that day*. In fact, Aaron does not explain the motive for his decision in any detail. Yet, at the end Moses seems to agree that Aaron may have acted properly.

Commentators assume that Aaron and his two surviving sons were permanently prohibited from mourning for the two who died. In this case the surviving sons are put under the same severe restriction as later high priests, perhaps because they too had been anointed. The restriction on the high priest is mentioned in 21:10–11. Later generations of ordinary priests were not anointed, and could mourn for immediate family members (21:1–4). Lev 10:7 is a stern warning to the priests to remain at their sanctuary duties.

At this point in Lev 10 there is no concern to have more purification offerings for the tabernacle area as a result of the deaths. In Lev 16 the purifications of Yom Kippur are the main focus, but the first verse of that chapter does mention the deaths of the two sons. Commentators suspect that Lev 16 may originally have followed Lev 10 and that the intervening five chapters were added at a later point.

Some of the main duties of priests outside the sanctuary are mentioned in 10:10-11. They are to *make distinctions* (*bdl*) between sacred and profane and between clean and unclean, and to teach all the laws to Israel. Ezekiel states the same most dramatically in Ezek 22:26. There the priests have *done violence* by not making the distinctions; they *profaned* holy things and because of this God's name *was profaned* among the people. The verb for *doing violence* (*hms*) is used in Gen 6:11, 13 to refer to the actions of sinful humanity before the flood.

The references to eating the grain offerings and the right breast and thigh of well-being offerings in Lev 10:12-15 may indicate that the proper portions of the offerings of the day had not yet been consumed by the priests. The reference to *any clean place* (10:14) could include the private residences of the priests and their families.

In 10:16 Moses raises the question of what happened to the people's purification offering. The verb form for *Moses made inquiry* is intensive; Milgrom translates the phrase as *Moses insistently inquired*. The same intensive form is used again in 10:18, *you should certainly have eaten it*.

The regulations in 6:24-30 indicate that priests are obligated to consume some or most of the meat from this category of sacrifice. The exception is for those animals whose blood is brought into the tabernacle to be used in major atonement rites. Those animal carcasses are to be burnt (6:30). Milgrom points out that the ingesting of the meat of this purification sacrifice is the heart of the ceremony. The priest can destroy the evil by eating the meat without any danger to himself.

The various references to purification offerings do not explain why all of them are not burnt, or why all of them cannot be eaten by the priests. One presupposition is that priests should not profit by consuming offerings for their own sins, but the logic to their being able to consume some of the meat from the people's offerings is never clearly spelled out.

After the plaint that *such things have happened* (*qra*) *to me*, Aaron asks if eating the sacrifice *would have been agreeable to the LORD*. The grammar of the Hebrew (*would it have been good in the eyes of the LORD?*)

indicates a strictly rhetorical question to which Aaron intends that the answer be in the negative. Moses then *agreed* with Aaron's conclusion; the Hebrew text says that *it was good in his eyes*. What is not spelled out for us is some of the logic behind Aaron's reply. All we know is that he somehow bases his actions on what had befallen him that day.

Milgrom notes that in the end Moses has the authority to challenge Aaron at any time, even though this case ends peacefully. Milgrom takes this as an example of the superiority of the role of a prophet over that of a priest.

Milgrom argues that there may be some complex history behind this story of the deaths of Nadab and Abihu. He suggests that the account may have been part of a polemic against pagan practices, specifically the private use of incense in the worship of astral deities. There are biblical references to such worship in Jer 19:13; 32:29; 44:17–19, 25; 2 Kgs 23:5, 12. Small portable incense tables were used; some were made of metal, some of brick or pottery. They were often set up on flat house rooftops. There are many archeological finds of these tables. Most of them are in the Assyrian religious style, perhaps influencing conquered lands such as Israel.

Stephen Sherwood takes the phrase about the unauthorized coals, *which he had not commanded them,* as an indirect reference to idolatry, since five of the other six times this phrase is used in the Old Testament have to do with idolatry. Sherwood and Milgrom mention that a minority of later rabbinic commentators thought that Nadab and Abihu could have been well-intentioned but overeager proponents of a legitimate form of worship, whose main mistake was in using the incense at an inappropriate time.

Milgrom notes that these ceremonies may not always have been idolatrous; perhaps some Israelites used these ceremonies to honor Yahweh in their own homes. There is a reference in Jer 41:5 about eighty men bringing incense to use at the site of the destroyed temple.

While prophets and other authorities usually condemned the practice as a slippery slope to idolatry, later on some rabbis seem to have been low-key about incense used privately to honor the LORD. Milgrom (630), going along with other historians, bluntly says "the rabbis were deliberately lenient in the matter of incense offerings because they knew full well that because they were widely practiced their prohibition would only be ignored."

Milgrom considers this story in Lev 10 as one more polemic against the private practice of using incense. In Exod 30:34–38 the authorized formula for incense in public worship is not to be used for any other purpose. In the Lev 10 account Nadab and Abihu used legitimate incense within the sanctuary, but they did not use embers taken from the altar as prescribed, but used *unauthorized* embers. Anyone using a private incense altar at home would have to use unauthorized coals; no one could snitch any from the high altar in the tabernacle or temple! Milgrom (631) calls this story "a perpetual reminder and threat to anyone else who would use *esh zarah* [*unauthorized embers*], all the more so because he or she would not be a priest, not with the proper incense, and not in the sanctuary."

With regard to the debate between Moses and Aaron, Milgrom says we need to focus on why eating the meat of this offering was so mandatory, and why Aaron felt that he and the other priests should not do so on this particular occasion.

In Lev 9:8–11 the blood of the priests' purification offerings was smeared on the horns of the altar and the rest of the animal was then burnt. As we suggested earlier, the animal may have been burnt because priests should not benefit from their own sacrifices. In 4:3–12 similar regulations are spelled out for inadvertent sins by the high priest himself. Perhaps these burnings, along with the ordination purification in Exod 29:10–14, represent an older custom. The unique, unrepeatable priestly consecrations and inauguration of the tabernacle may have been understood as the last examples of the old custom.

Milgrom suggests that later on the new custom was that if the sacrificial blood was used only on the outer altar then the priests were to eat the meat themselves.

In this case in Lev 10, because of the wrongs done by Nadab and Abihu, and the contamination brought on by their corpses within the tabernacle area, Aaron and his sons decided that this purification offering was as serious as the inadvertent sins in Lev 4 or the annual requirements of Yom Kippur, so this offering of the people should be burnt instead.

So we are looking at a borderline case, with Moses on one side and Aaron on the other. In the end they agree to disagree, which might represent a victory or point of honor for Aaron in the eyes of Priestly editors.

Questions

23. What do you find upsetting about 10:1–7?
24. Does this story of a major sin have any parallels in Exodus? Explain.
25. As Moses remarked in 10:17–18, the normal procedure for a purification offering for the people was that the priests themselves ate of the meat after the blood had been used to cleanse the main altar. The evil thus removed was imagined to remain within the body of the sacrificed animal. Can you explain the theology behind this procedure?
26. If you were to judge 10:16–20 without any detailed knowledge of the rules about what should be burnt and what should be eaten by the priests, what impressions would you have about Moses and Aaron?

Conclusion

In commenting on the role of the priests as teachers in Lev 10:10–11, Milgrom offers a clear profile of the unity between priests and people. The priests are not the recipients of private revelations; both priests and people are taught all the rules and regulations. The priests are to teach and uphold these practices, but they are not the guardians of secret arts. As we read in Deut 33:4, "Moses charged us with the law, as a possession for the assembly of Jacob."

Leviticus 11:1—16:54

Section Eleven

Leviticus 11:1—15:33

The mention of Nadab and Abihu in 16:1 is taken by scholars as an indication that Lev 16 may have originally followed Lev 10. The mention of *clean* and *unclean* in 10:10 may also serve as a notice that chs. 11–15 will now serve as examples which we can use to appreciate the annual rites of atonement on Yom Kippur, the subject of Lev 16.

For the sake of continuity, I ask readers to plow through all of chs. 11–15 now, at one sitting if possible. Particulars of the following brief outline will then be reviewed, with questions interspersed.

Brief Overview of Leviticus 11–15

Lev 11 lists various *clean* and *unclean* creatures. The clean group includes animals that have divided hooves, cleft feet, and are ruminants, or cud chewers. This limits the Israelites to using cattle, sheep, and goats for meat. Four exceptions are the camel, rock badger, hare, and pig, all considered unclean. Fish with fins and scales are allowed, but not shellfish. Several predatory bird species are banned, as are most insects, with the exception of locusts and grasshoppers. Wild animals with paws are also banned, as are rodents, lizards, and other amphibians. Some simple purification rites are then outlined, such as washing one's clothing and breaking clay pottery that has been tainted. Swarming insects and reptiles are also banned.

Question

27. Assuming that the classes of clean and unclean creatures make sense on some level, pick out the most notable or puzzling two pairs of verses in Lev 11.

Lev 12 describes periods of ceremonial uncleanness for women after childbirth. The mother of a newborn son must avoid touching anything designated for use at the sanctuary, and not visit the sanctuary herself for seven days, and then again for another thirty-three days after the boy's circumcision. These two periods represent the average spans for serious and minor bleeding episodes following childbirth. This span of forty days is doubled when the newborn is a daughter. The chapter ends with prescribed offerings after the forty or eighty days.

Question

28. How normal a life could a new mother live during these forty or eighty days? Why is the time span doubled for having a daughter? Why is atonement mentioned in 12:7–8?

Lev 13 describes disfiguring skin eruptions. Milgrom calls them *scale diseases*, where skin or scab elements are shed. The older English use of the word *leprosy* is very inexact. The disfiguring symptoms don't correspond to Hanson's disease, the modern term for leprosy itself. The person with the skin eruption undergoes one or more weeklong periods of quarantine at home, followed by inspections by a priest. One odd exemption (13:12–13) is mentioned: when a person's whole body turns white. From our point of view this indicates the serious advancement of some disease, but the uniformity of the white color seems to fit the definition of cleanness in some way. The chapter goes on about the white color of the skin, boils, burn marks, hair discolored by underlying skin ailments, rashes, etc. We are assured that baldness does not count as a problem (13:40–41). The one mention that some people with scale disease may need to live outside the camp comes in 13:45–46. The chapter ends with procedures for treating molds or fungi that can settle in wool, linen ,or leather clothing.

Questions

29. What is going on in Lev 13?

30. What style or thrust do Lev 11–13 have in common?

Lev 14 details the ceremonies needed when one is declared clean of a scale disease. Two wild birds are used; one is sacrificed and the other is then released to fly off to its remote habitat. The cleansed person goes through a weeklong period of living next to his or her tent, and then is marked with blood and oil before moving back inside.

The next topic is molds or fungi that settle into plaster, mud, or stone walls. The various periods of inspection, quarantine, and replacement of sections of a wall follow logically from what we have seen so far. In rare cases an entire house might have to be demolished. A simple ceremony using two wild birds is called for at the end of these procedures. One odd item is that the homeowner is advised to remove all furniture from the affected rooms so that the priest can do his examining (14:36). There seems to be no concern that molds or fungi could be settling in the furniture as well.

Question

31. What are we looking at in 14:1–20?

Lev 15 speaks of abnormal discharges of mucus or blood from the genital organs of men or women. People with these problems must make sure that no one touches the beds or chairs that they use. The uncleanness in these cases is purely ceremonial. Quarantines and washings are prescribed, and then small offerings at the sanctuary. The editors mention normal discharges of semen (including marital intercourse), normal menstruation, and the occasional problem of prolonged bleeding after menstruation. The only verse that provides a motive for these situations of cleanness or uncleanness is 15:31, which speaks of the need to avoid defiling the sanctuary.

Questions

32. What is the point of 15:11? Should there be a parallel verse associated with 15:19–27?

33. What is your overall reaction or impression after reading Lev 11–15?

Further Details and Questions

Perhaps we can learn from the details as to how the category of uncleanness functioned. We could also look at other ancient Near Eastern cultures for hints, and, finally, we should look for positive dimensions of this piety.

Leviticus 11

Milgrom notes the blending of various Priestly sources in Lev 11. He argues for a second hand in 11:24–38, where purification rites are listed, and in 11:47, a second postscript. He finds a third hand in 11:39–40, perhaps the final layer of editing. The call to be holy as God is holy in 11:43–45 is clearly in the Holiness style of chs. 17–27.

The editing scheme for Lev 11 could be outlined as follows. Milgrom calls all of 11:24–40 a section that "sticks out like a sore thumb," with its different subject matter.

11:1–2	Introduction
11:2–8	Quadrupeds
11:9–12	Fish
11:13–19	Birds
11:20–23	Flying insects
11:24–28	Rules about forbidden quadrupeds P2
11:29–38	Rules about land swarmers P2
11:39–40	Rules about permitted quadrupeds P3
11:41–42	Other land swarmers
11:43–45	Call to holiness H
11:46	Postscript
11:47	Postscript P2

Deut 14:3–20 (especially 4–8) seems to be modeled after Lev 11. A few more non-sacrificial animals are mentioned, mainly game animals.

Within Lev 11 *detestable* things cannot be eaten, but do not pollute the sanctuary, while *unclean* things cannot be eaten and do pollute. The cultic terms *unclean* (*tma*) and *detestable* (*shqz*) derive from nouns, but to *regard as detestable* (11:11) comes from the related verb *shqz*; it can also mean to *make yourself detestable*, as in 11:43. The parallel term in 11:44, *do not defile yourselves*, is from its related verb *tma*. To *be clean* is from the Hebrew verb *thr*, often used with regard to cultic points.

Milgrom notes that the use of the verb *shqz* in 11:43 matches the phrase *you shall not bring abomination upon yourselves* in 22:25–26. The generalizations in 11:43–45 are broader than the rest of the chapter, and point to the Holiness source. He remarks:

> For H, which enjoins the attainment of holiness upon all Israel, the diet laws are indispensable, not just as a heuristic and disciplinary regimen but as a constitutive and integral element of holiness itself. As impurity and holiness are antithetic states, Israel can *eo ipso* not be holy if it defiles itself with impure forces. The result of such defilement is also spelled out: expulsion from the land. . . This notion that Israel's land tenure is dependent on its collective practice of separation and holiness is solely the teaching of H. (689)

Milgrom starts his analysis of Lev 11 by looking at the animal blood prohibition which lies behind the listing of clean and unclean animals (see Lev 3 [esp. v. 17]; 7:22–27; 17:10–14). In these passages the blood of sacrificed animals must be dashed against the altar and not consumed; other clean animals for the table should have their blood returned to the earth and covered, but that blood should not be consumed. Similar rules can be found in Deut 26.

The origin of these procedures regarding the blood of animals can be traced to Gen 9:1–6. When God gave Noah permission to eat meat as well as plants, he demanded respect for the life forces in the blood of animals, and promised to punish humans who murdered other humans. Note the references to *all flesh* in Gen 6:12–13, where the phrase refers to human beings, and perhaps also to predatory animals.

Milgrom differs with the traditional translation of Gen 9:6, *whoever sheds the blood of a human, by a human shall that person's blood be shed*. Milgrom argues that both references to a human refer to the victim, and that the phrase *by a human* would be better translated *in exchange for a human*. The full verse would be *Whoever sheds the blood of a human, in exchange for a human shall that person's blood be shed; for in his own image God created mankind*. This fits in with Gen 9:5, where God takes the responsibility for punishing for murder and for balancing the acts of violence done by or against animals. Milgrom notes that these blood prohibitions apply to all of humanity, whereas some of the Ten Commandments apply only to Israel as a covenant partner.

Note the word *only* (or *however*) at the start of Gen 9:4. Here God is altering the original plan that humans would only eat plants. Milgrom argues that the narrowing of choices of meat to specific herd animals, properly slaughtered, may have helped control cruelty, the killer instinct in humans hinted at in Gen 9:2, "The fear and dread of you shall rest on every animal of the earth, and on every bird of the air, on everything that creeps on the ground, and on all the fish of the sea; into your hand they are delivered." Milgrom takes the covering of animal blood by earth as part of this sensitivity to the slaughter of animals for food.

There seem to be no ancient Near Eastern parallel customs about the proper shedding of blood in animal sacrifices, nor any ban on ingesting blood, yet the Priestly view is that this ethic should apply to all human beings. As one example, in Lev 17 resident aliens are required to follow this rule. Lev 17:3–4 nearly equates unauthorized animal slaughter to murder, and 17:11 speaks of sacrificial blood as a form of atonement: "For the life of the flesh is in the blood; and I have given it to you for making atonement for your lives on the altar; for, as life, it is the blood that makes atonement." Milgrom understands blood as the divinely instituted force in all animal and human life, the only force that can drive out impurity and the realm of death.

Milgrom reminds us that Priestly traditions about animals are extensive. Like a human, an animal has a *nefesh* (*soul*). In Gen 1:20, 21, 24, 30 animals are called *living creatures* (*nefesh hayya*); the same term refers to humans alone in Gen 2:7 as *living beings*. Animals that kill humans may be covered by the phrases in Gen 9:5, mentioned earlier. In Exod 21:28–32 an ox that kills a person must be stoned, and its flesh may not be eaten under any circumstances. Lev 20:15–16 calls for the death of any animal misused in bestiality. Livestock are not to work on the Sabbath (Exod 20:10). To end on a lighter note, readers will remember the peaceable kingdom passage in Isa 11:6–9, where animals and humans will again live in a peaceful, vegetarian world.

Milgrom speaks of a Priestly uneasiness regarding man's uncontrolled power over animal life. He speculates that this unease goes far back into human history, as ancient hunters and herdsmen sought to placate minor divinities that ruled over animal life. Milgrom notes that Priestly traditions turned this into an ethical imperative. In his final remarks on the blood prohibition he notes that while everyone now has a right to the nourishment meat provides, the draining and covering of animal blood rightly returns this symbol of life to God's realm.

Rabbis later specified a correct slaughtering process: using the sharpest blade, and cleanly and swiftly cutting the carotids and trachea entirely to induce rapid and painless unconsciousness.

Let us go on to some other details in Lev 11. Two older theories have been used to explain the division between clean and unclean animals. Some have raised the question of diseases, such as trichinosis in pigs, and others have taken some animals to act improperly or at least oddly (such as crawling crustaceans).

Milgrom suggests that we could start by simply agreeing that customs and rituals reflect a society's values. We have already seen some of the Priestly respect for clean animals, and the closing chapters of Job offer a moving overview of God's interest in the natural world. Another strong passage is found in 20:22–26. Milgrom (725) comments on this vocational call in Lev 20, "What could be clearer! Israel's attainment of holiness is dependent on setting itself apart from the nations and the prohibited animal foods. The dietary system is thus a reflection and reinforcement of Israel's election."

Setting oneself apart must also include coming closer to something else. Here separation from the nations is a positive concept, an inspiration and a goal associated with God's nature and his desire for contact with us. Coming closer to God must also include ethics, and related food customs as part of this ethic. Milgrom reminds us that

> the holy may never become impure. These two categories are antagonistic, totally opposite. They are antonyms. Moreover, they are dynamic: they seek to extend their influence and control over the other two categories, the common and the pure. In contrast to the former, the latter two categories are static. They cannot transfer their state; there is no contagious purity or contagious commonness. Indeed, they are, in effect, secondary

> categories. They take their identity from their antonyms. Purity is the absence of impurity; commonness is the absence of holiness. . . . Hence, the boundaries between the holy and the common and between the pure and the impure . . . [are not] fixed. . . . Israel by its behavior can move the boundaries—either way. But it is enjoined to move in one direction only: *to advance the holy* into the realm of the common and *to diminish the impure* and thereby enlarge the realm of the pure. (732)

The dietary system, with its significant limitations of meat and fish, has as its purpose to teach reverence for life as a gift from God and to promote the custom of humane slaughter.

When delving further in Lev 11, we find it difficult to explain the classification of each and every animal. Milgrom suggests that in some cases a classification might have originally been rooted in opposition to idolatrous practices in nearby cultures, as implied in 20:22-26. Other underlying motives might have involved aesthetics, concepts about hygiene, or taboos for which no one can now identify the ancient roots.

Question

34. What would be the result of avoiding shellfish, as found in the prohibitions of 11:10-12?

The camel was correctly identified as not having hooves. The rock badger and hare are not ruminants; biblical traditions misread the sideways chewing motions of the animals as cud chewing. The pig is not a ruminant. Milgrom assumes that the category of cud chewing was deliberately chosen in order to eliminate the pig from the list of clean animals. In Hittite and Philistine cultures the pig was the sacrificial animal of choice for honoring certain underworld deities and demons. Thus pigs were likely avoided because of their use in polytheistic rites.

The swarming ground insects of 11:41-43 may have been considered so earth bound (burrowing, hiding under rocks or rotting vegetation etc.) that they were associated with the underworld forces of death. Lev 11:44 contrasts the holiness of God with the defilement by these ground insects.

Leviticus 12

Most likely the new mother was to keep track of the days involved in these regulations. Milgrom assumes there were ablutions at the end of the seven- or fourteen-day spans, although they are not mentioned. After the initial span of the week or two, the woman could return to all her day-to-day duties. When the longer period of forty or eighty days ended, she could return to the sanctuary with everyone else. The intent of these quarantines seems to be entirely ritual, and not a judgment about any personal sins. Rabbis later applied these rules to the case of mothers of stillborn infants.

Ancients assumed that a woman's generative elements were within her blood in some way (not understanding the system of the ova and fallopian tubes). Many ancient Near Eastern cultures isolated new mothers (and menstruating women as well) to a greater degree than we have in the Old Testament. In some cultures the newborn infant had to be excluded from religious ceremonies for a period as well.

The reference in 12:3 to infant circumcision does intrude on the main topic of the chapter. Circumcision rites for males in many ancient cultures seem to have originally been associated with passage to adulthood or marriage. At some point Israelites apparently moved this rite to infancy and associated it more closely with covenant theology.

Questions

35. Why do you think new mothers were considered ceremonially unclean for these periods of forty or eighty days?
36. In Luke 2:22–24 Joseph and Mary took Jesus to the temple after his circumcision "when the time came for their purification according to the law of Moses." Why is the phrase for their purification in the plural, since in Leviticus and elsewhere only the mother had to undergo the forty days of absence from the sanctuary?

Leviticus 13

Milgrom prefers to call these *scale diseases* (*zraat*)—ones generating scabs or flakes, something like psoriasis or fungal infections. Some of the white skin conditions might occur immediately after scabs or crusts fall off. In some cases there is minor bleeding associated with the disturbing or falling away of these scabs, which could explain the *raw flesh* mentioned at several points in the chapter.

Question

37. Have you ever experienced skin symptoms such as these, or known others who have?

Despite 13:46, Milgrom questions where those with these scale diseases had to live. They could not live at home because that house would become unclean; perhaps they stayed in tent camps within or outside the community. The logic for the quarantines seems to be entirely ritual—almost at the corpse-contamination level. Some fear of contagion might have been in the popular mind, even if not officially adopted by the Priestly tradition. In fact, many of these skin conditions were not contagious.

Milgrom suggests that instead of further speculation on the chronic skin conditions and their complex symptoms, we should rather remember the Priestly logic behind chs. 13–14. The focus is on *purity* or *cleanness* over against *impurity* or *uncleanness*. Root forms of *clean* appear thirty-six times in the two chapters, and forms of *unclean* appear thirty times. At only four locations (13:18, 37; 14:3, 48) is the verb to *heal* (*rpa*) used, and the last refers to the *healing* of the walls of a house.

What is described in detail is the inspection of the appearance of the skin diseases, and changes in those appearances. Appearance is also what links the notion of molds in fabric or plaster, adobe, and stone to the larger context. The Old Testament rarely mentions the progress of physical illnesses within most organs, and possible cures for them, in comparison to many ancient Near Eastern cultures. In later centuries rabbis clearly exempted non-Jews (and their dwellings) from all these scale disease regulations, and also exempted the houses of Jewish people who lived abroad. The concern is that any Israelite who is unclean because of these conditions should avoid contact with holy items and should not attend ceremonies at the sanctuary.

Milgrom notes that the ritual focus on scale diseases makes sense if we take them as aspects of death, as in the wasting away of the skin of a stillborn or of an ordinary corpse. He points to the story of Miriam's punishment, climaxing in Num 12:12, and to the remark of Bildad concerning sinners in Job 18:13.

Leviticus 14

Milgrom outlines chs. 13–14 in this way, assigning the matter of discoloration of fabrics to a second Priestly editor. Note stylistic differences in 14:33–53. The first-person statement in 14:34 and the mention there of coming into Canaan and having possessions, the wordy style in parts of 14:36, 39, 41, 43–45, and the more well-developed chiasms are all indicative of editing by the later priestly Holiness school.

P1	13:1–46	Scale disease examinations
	14:1–32	Rites after healing
P2	13:47–59	Fungal growths in fabric (summary in v. 59)
H	14:33–53	Fungal growths in walls, and final rites
	14:54–57	Summary

Lev 14:3 mentions the priest making his examination *outside the camp*, perhaps echoing 13:45–46. The person with the ailment must remain outside the camp until the examination is completed. Lev 14:2 mentions *cleansing* or *purification*, but the context makes it clear that the person has already been healed before these ceremonies take place. Strictly speaking, 14:3 says that "the scale disease has been healed *of* (or *in*) the scale-diseased person." This could also be rendered "the scale disease has *disappeared from* the scale-diseased person."

Question

38. The ceremony with two wild birds in 14:4–7 is somewhat unusual; while the one is sacrificed, the other is freed at the end. Cedar chips and red yarn seem like odd ingredients. What do you think is the theology behind all the details?

The healed person could now return to the camp, but must live outside his or her own tent for seven days, completing that period with a second round of laundering, shaving, and bathing. The seven days outside the tent is to prevent contamination by overhang (spreading within an enclosed space).

Question

39. The ceremonies outlined in 14:10–20 are quite extensive. How do you think the individual felt by the end?

Other ancient Near Eastern cultures took fungal infections in the walls of houses to be demonic. The Priestly traditions modified this to simple examinations and purifications. Later on, rabbis suggested that these damaging growths might have been brought on by personal sins, but they exempted non-Jewish homes and all homes outside the Holy Land from such inspections. Their only concern was for any impurity reaching the sanctuary.

Milgrom reminds us that in Israel priests were not involved in any other medical cases except scale disease (see Deut 24:8–9). In Lev 15, on genital discharges, the ones suffering do all the reporting of their ordeals; the priests accept their sacrifices as needed. We should not think of priests as health officers; even the skin diseases mentioned here do not seem to be contagious in general.

Further, the ceremonies do not bring about cure; they only help the healed individual regain full status within the community of worshipers. Milgrom (888) notes, "The disease is not a demonic entity independent of God, nor is the ritual an intrinsically effective agency of healing. Both disease and healing stem from the one God. The ritual, bereft of its inherent power, is transformed into a symbolic purification; it becomes a religious, and not a therapeutic act."

The discoloration and disfigurement caused by scale diseases endangered the sanctuary and the community of worshipers, even if confined to a few individuals. The sacrifices, and related shaving and bathing, were part of the ritual battle between the forces of life and death, holiness and impurity.

Milgrom refers to the healed individual as the *celebrant* of this battle. I'm sure he means that the individual presides at the ceremony in an important way, and that he is not using the word simply to refer to someone who is happy to be healed of his or her scale disease. Milgrom's summary is a fitting way to end this scene: "Thus the entire purification process is nothing but a ritual, a rite of passage, marking the transition from death to life. As the celebrant moves from the realm of impurity outside the camp, restored first to his community, then to his home, and finally to his sanctuary, he has passed from impurity to holiness, from death to life, is reinstated with his family, and is reconciled with his God" (889).

Within Herod's renovated temple there was an outdoor enclosure for healed scale-diseased people to bathe by immersion before presenting these eighth-day sacrifices. This immersion was in addition to the laundering, shaving, and bathing mentioned above, and represented a new stage of ritual beyond Leviticus. Later on, rabbis added the requirement of another immersion after presenting the sacrifices.

Leviticus 15

Milgrom outlines this Priestly chapter as a chiasm, a structure that has matching pairs of ideas or images arranged before and after a midpoint. Here 15:18 serves as the midpoint, introducing the switch from rules for men to rules for women.

15:1	Introduction
15:2–15	Abnormal male secretions
15:16–18	Normal male secretions, including relations with wife (18 serves as an interlocking hinge in the chiastic structure)
15:19–24	Normal female secretions (menstruation)
15:25–30	Abnormal female secretions (bleeding)
15:31	Mention of the tabernacle or sanctuary
15:32–33	Summary

The male secretions in Lev 15:2–15 may refer to mucus generated by *gonorrhea benigna*, a milder form of the current disease. It was not contagious except by sexual contact, and the man could reside at home for the duration. This seems to be a change from the strictures of Num 5:1–3 and Deut 23:10–11.

Later rabbis sought to reestablish some of the broader commands in those chapters.

Lev 15:18 follows 15:16–17 grammatically. The reference to a woman or wife anticipates the next few paragraphs.

Question

40. Why would normal marital relations be considered unclean, even for the time needed for bathing and sunset, as in 15:18?

In many ancient cultures menstruating women were moved to isolation and were even feared; evil forces were thought to inhabit their blood secretions. The regulations in Leviticus are quite mild by comparison. Milgrom points out that an Israelite woman could touch others in the course of her ordinary home duties. Family members simply avoided the use of her chair and bed or taking the initiative to touch her.

Strictly speaking, there were rules against deliberate relations with a menstruating woman (as in 20:18 and elsewhere), but in 15:24 the focus seems to be narrow, concerned only with the level of the impurity.

In many other cultures holy water in myths and rituals was thought to magically vivify as well as purify. In Israel water was simply a means for purification, as set out in divine commands. Note that ablutions took place only *after* healing had already taken place, and there were never any prayer formulas used during the bathing.

The special water given to the suspected adulteress in Num 5 was really part of what Milgrom calls "a cooling off process." Num 5:21 specifically notes that God will send down the punishment; the power is not in the water itself.

Milgrom notes the almost universal taboos on close contact with menstruants, calling them a worldwide male psychological phenomenon.

The few restrictions on menstruants in Lev 15 are lenient by comparison, but Milgrom provides evidence that many Israelite men were not inclined to be as lenient. Later rabbis (after 70 CE) sought to transfer some of the ideals of sanctuary holiness to individual households, and additional restrictions on menstruants were part of that movement.

Milgrom (953) notes that in biblical times most Israelite women rarely had the time for regular menstrual periods, with early marriage, frequent pregnancies, and the duty of nursing each infant for more than two years. He postulates that women "were rarely excluded from participating in the cult" because of Lev 15.

We have noted Milgrom's conviction that the Priestly traditions removed demonic forces from their role in battling other gods, even as the editors kept the notion that people in unclean or sinful states did offend God and defile his sanctuary.

Section Eleven

Questions

41. Consider for a moment the span of topics in Lev 11–15. How do you think customs such as these could help ordinary people have a closer relationship with God?

42. Setting aside for the moment short-term exclusions from the sanctuary such as required for new mothers or men and women with abnormal secretions, how do you think those with long-term conditions felt about having to stay away from sanctuary gatherings for years at a time? Were those who could not even stay at home kept busy? Could they play any role to help their families or their nation?

43. After describing in detail the conditions in Lev 13 and the cleansing rites of Lev 14, Roland de Vaux, a scholar from the 1940s and 50s, concludes:

    All these various prescriptions are evidence of very primitive ideas; they are the remains of old superstitious rites. And yet there is no reference to them in the pre-exilic texts, just as there is no reference to the ashes of the red heifer or to the use of lustral water in the years before the Exile. There is only one possible conclusion, and it must apply to all the laws about purity in Lev 11–16: after the Exile, the Jews became increasingly conscious of the need for purity, and the fear of impurity became an obsession with them; hence the writers of the Priests' Code multiplied the instances of impurity and prescribed all the correct remedies for it; they borrowed material on every side, integrated popular superstitions into the Levitical system and proposed so many prescriptions that the law became too complicated to be practical. Post-biblical Judaism traveled even farther in the same direction. The ritual had at first given expression to the holiness of God and of his people, but it changed into a narrow system of formal observance, a yoke too heavy to be borne; what had once been a protection became an iron collar. (463–64)

    Are his conclusions convincing, or are they subject to debate?

Conclusion

E. P. Sanders, in his book *Judaism: Practice and Belief, 63 BCE–66 CE* (212–30), argues persuasively that many of these pious customs mentioned in Leviticus and Numbers were still observed by Jewish people during the lifetime of Jesus. He notes the practical limitations for Jewish people who lived far from the land of Israel, and the gradual addition within Israel of immersion pools and more frequent washing of clothing, etc., which went beyond the biblical regulations themselves. Sanders concludes:

> The very wide distribution of immersion pools, so strikingly demonstrated by archaeology, shows that the purity laws were generally obeyed. It should be especially emphasized that archaeologists have found miqva'ot [immersion pools] wherever they have explored substantial remains from the late second temple period. We should not go beyond the Pharisees and rabbis and accuse the ordinary people of not obeying the purity laws. On the contrary, a lot of Palestinian Jews accepted more purity rules than the Bible requires, as we saw when we discussed handling the priests' food.
>
> Modern critics of ancient Judaism often find all this objectionable. Often it is said that only the Pharisees developed and cared about purity laws, a supposition that assists the criticism of Pharisaism as being externalistic and trivial. In fact, purifications were common to all ancient religions. Pagans washed their hands before sacrificing and dipped their hands or sprinkled themselves before entering a temple. All groups within Judaism purified themselves in various ways; there was also a distinct tendency to invent new purifications or to extend the biblical laws beyond their original sphere. We see again that the Judaism of our period was an ancient religion. Its external observances were different from those of other religions in detail, not in kind. Jews and Gentiles disagreed about a lot of things: about pork, but not about whether or not dietary laws were appropriate; about the Sabbath, but not about the importance of holy days. Had they debated it, pagans would have argued against Palestinian Jews that immersion was stupid; one should sprinkle and dip.
>
> Thoughtful ancient people, however, whether Jew or Gentile, interpreted their rituals as the external expression of piety, not

as a substitute for it. A rite was a rite and what mattered was what it stood for. (229–30)

Section Twelve

LEVITICUS 16:1–34

Note: Most of the questions for Lev 16 will be placed right after the outline of the verses.

Lev 16 describes a complex array of sacrifices and prayers intended to purify the tabernacle (or temple) and to bring forgiveness for all of Israel's sins. The spiritual purposes of this annual holyday are still observed at Yom Kippur, the Day of Atonement, which is one of the most important days in the modern synagogue calendar. The verb to *atone* (*kpr*) is used often throughout the chapter. The sequence of steps is a bit confusing, but not impossible to follow. A simple outline can be given here.

The priest has to do different things in three different locations. First, he enters the holy of holies, the inmost room of the tabernacle. The NRSV calls this the *sanctuary* or *holy place*, or speaks of the priest coming *inside the curtain*, which marks off this area containing the ark of the covenant with its gold cover (*kapporet*, traditionally translated as the *mercy seat*). In the centuries after the ark was lost, the inner room was completely empty, but was still revered as the focal point of God's presence.

The outer room of the tabernacle is called the *tent of meeting*, where a metal incense table was the most important fixture. Finally, some ceremonies take place at the main altar, in the courtyard outside the tent itself.

Commentators raise many questions about ancient Near Eastern parallels to the scapegoat rite, and note that other cultures strove to purify and safeguard their temples from demonic forces or rival deities. They also study the complex vocabulary used here, and supply some of the logical sequences that were left unexplained in the text. We can benefit from some of these findings, but we should keep in mind that the topic of sin and repentance is most worthy of our study.

Milgrom prefers to identify the *sin offerings* as *purification offerings*, as we have seen elsewhere. For *kpr* he uses noun and verb phrases from *purgation* and *to purge*, arguing that the words *to atone* and *atonement* are more puzzling than helpful in most of this chapter. He does translate *kpr* in 16:10 as to *perform expiation*, and in 16:24 he uses *atonement* exactly as the NRSV. Milgrom notes that the verb *kpr* has a broad range of meanings.

16:1	Introduction
16:2–5	Aaron is to wear linen vestments, and to bring a bull as a sin offering for the priests, and a ram as their burnt offering. He also brings two male goats as sin offerings for the people, and one ram as their burnt offering.
16:6–10	One of the two male goats is chosen by lot to be the regular sin offering, and the other is designated for Azazel (ancient versions translated this as scapegoat, but modern translators prefer to take it as a proper name).
16:11–14	After slaughtering the bull, Aaron incenses the holy place, and places some of the blood on and near the mercy seat.
16:15–17	Aaron repeats these procedures at the mercy seat with the blood of the male goat chosen as the regular sin offering. Then he apparently uses blood from the bull and the goat for the same purposes within the tent of meeting, placing the blood on and near the incense altar.
16:18–19	A combination of blood from the bull and the goat is then put on and around the horns of the main altar in the courtyard.

16:20-22   Aaron puts both hands on the head of the Azazel goat, and pronounces the sins of Israel over it. The goat, now in some sense bearing all these sins, is led to a wilderness area. There is no mention of the goat's fate, but it should not leave the wilderness.

16:23-28   Aaron now bathes and changes into more formal vestments, and sacrifices the two rams as burnt offerings at the altar, as well as the fat portions of the sin offerings. Details are added about the return of the person who took the Azazel goat to the wilderness, and we learn that the carcasses of the bull and goat used in the sin offerings had to be taken outside the camp and totally incinerated.

16:29-34   A parallel passage from H (Holiness editors, a later branch of P) provides details about all of Israel abstaining from work on this annual holyday, and denying themselves (perhaps by fasting). The word atonement is used six times in these verses. The style of this passage is clearly different from 16:2-28.

Questions

44. If you were to read Lev 16 immediately after Lev 10, how would 16:1-5 strike you?
45. Look at the instructions in 16:3-10. How does 16:11 move the chapter along?
46. If Lev 16 ended with v. 15, what do you learn from the use of the incense and blood sprinkling in 16:11-15?
47. How does the one verse 16:16 assist the reader?
48. Why is the altar hallowed (or reconsecrated) in 16:19, when the holy of holies and the tent of meeting are not?
49. Why do we come back to the scapegoat in 16:20?
50. How can anyone "put sins on the head" of an animal? Why does this ceremony make any sense at all?

51. Burnt offerings are usually acts of adoration. Why do they contribute to atonement in 16:23-25?

52. Why must the bull and first goat carcasses be incinerated outside the camp?

53. Note some of the style differences in 16:29-34 as compared to the rest of the chapter.

Taking 16:2-28 as a unit, some of the vocabulary is unusual. Aaron is *not to come just at any time* into the sanctuary inside the curtain. The Hebrew in 16:2 can also mean *at all times*. If we look back at 10:1-7, the death of Aaron's two sons came about because they had committed sacrilege before the LORD. The ceremonies in Lev 16 may reflect ancient traditions about purifying the entire tabernacle area in emergencies; such would have been needed right at that aftermath of sacrilege and death. Rabbis suggested that Aaron could enter beyond the curtain as needed (for instance, after the death of his sons), but that his successors could only enter there once a year (as we first learn in 16:29).

In Lev 16 the inmost room is consistently called the *holy place* (*qodesh*), while in all other Priestly sources the inmost room is called the *holy of holies* (*qodesh haqqodeshim*) and *holy place* refers to the outer room. Likewise, only in Lev 16 does the term *tent of meeting* refer just to the outer room of the tabernacle; elsewhere it refers to the entire tent or shrine. The word *transgression* is used in P only in 16:16, 21. These unusual vocabulary choices could be further indications that 16:2-28 was received as a complete unit by the editors.

Clearly the use of a scapegoat may have developed from ancient exorcisms. In those rites evil was banished to a place of isolation or to a place where it could trouble the original spiritual being who sent it. *Azazel* has been associated with verbal roots that come close to *scapegoat* or *rough wilderness place*. The more recent theory is that it was an ancient proper name of a long-forgotten demon or satyr. Choosing the destiny of each male goat by lot left the choice up to God. In this way the high priest would not be mistaken as the one initiating the use of the scapegoat in any connection with a demon or minor deity.

We should think of the goat simply as a vehicle for moving the sins. Milgrom remarks that Azazel himself has no active role; he neither receives the goat nor attacks it. In the Priestly ritual he is no longer a personality but just a name, designating the place to which impurities and sins are banished. Milgrom (1024) cites T. H. Gaster: "demons often survive as figures of speech (e.g., 'gremlins') long after they have ceased to be figures of belief. Accordingly, the mention of a demon's name in a scriptural text is not automatic testimony to living belief in him."

In 16:9 Aaron offers the people's goat for the *sin* or *purification* sacrifice on the assumption that some of their sins were brazen. Therefore they could not present their own sacrificial animals. The remarks in Num 15:30–31 indicate that those whose sins were so bold as to be blasphemous were to be shunned (*cut off*); thus they could not simply come to the sanctuary whenever they wished. That passage speaks of individuals *acting high-handedly, affronting the LORD*, and of having *despised the word of the LORD*. The phrase *high-handedly* (*beyad ramah, with a high hand*) is found in Exod 14:8, which describes the Israelites at the Red Sea intent on leaving Egypt with this exact attitude. The same phrase is repeated in Num 33:3. In both cases the NRSV uses the word *boldly*, which might be a bit weak. The Hebrew term certainly implies premeditation. See also Lev 6:1–7, which speaks of making complete restitution for injustices before bringing guilt offerings to the priests.

The *atonement* (*kapper*) or *expiation* in Lev 16:10 is performed upon the *Azazel* goat in the sense that the purgation of the sanctuary will be completed when the goat, laden with the sanctuary's impurities, is dispatched to the wilderness. Looking ahead to 16:21–22, we can say that the sins of the people will also be removed, provided they enact their remorse through acts of self-denial and cessation from labor. Using the word *atonement* or *expiation* in 16:10 is justified because the author is looking at the bigger picture, the impact of the community's repentance.

The purpose of incense is to honor God. It was also used one time to ward off a plague, as we see in Aaron's use of the censor in Num 16:45–50.

In Lev 16:12–13 it seems that the priest is to light the incense after going past the curtain. If so, the priest would have risked seeing the ark itself for a minute. Milgrom notes that the *cloud* of incense in 16:13 (and perhaps in 16:2) would not have provided a dense enough shield to protect the priest from close contact with the Divine Presence, unless smoke-enhancing compounds were used along with the incense. Such compounds are mentioned in rabbinic sources, which suggested that a smoke enhancer was used to prevent this exposure to the ark. The enhancer was lit by the high priest just before entering the holy place, and then he lit the incense just after coming inside. Their point was that incense was used for honoring or placating God; it never had the primary purpose of providing a screen or shield.

As we work our way through this chapter, learning the fine details of the rituals, 16:16 provides the first explanation that the atonement is needed for the *uncleanness* (*tumot*) of the sanctuary and for the *transgressions* (*pshy*) and *sins* (*hta*) of the people.

The word *uncleanness* is used twice in this verse, and drives home the point that sin and error dishonor God's sanctuary. The remark that the *tent of meeting remains with them in the midst of their uncleannesses* is really a reference to God abiding with them despite their failures.

The word *transgressions* is based on a verb meaning to *rebel*. It refers to the worst possible sins. These sins can be against other people, as Jacob challenged Laban in Gen 31:36, "what is my *offense*?" The same term can refer to rebellion against God, as in Jer 5:6, "their *transgressions* are many, their apostasies are great." We should reflect again on Num 15:27–31, which contrasts the use of *sin offerings* for unintentional wrongs with the shunning of those who have despised the word of the LORD and broken his commandments.

In 16:17 no one accompanies the high priest when he is within the tent; this may represent how dangerous it is for anyone to approach God's presence.

With all the areas purged, the impurities and sins can now be set upon the scapegoat. Aaron places both hands on the animal and makes a proclamation to signify this transfer of all that is evil. A somewhat similar proclamation can be found in 5:5 (and assumed in 6:1–7).

In this passage the focus is on the sins, not on the sanctuary pollution. The twofold mention of *uncleanness* (*tumot*) in 16:16 is paralleled by the use of *iniquities* (*awon*) in 16:21–22. Both words are used to summarize what is going on. Blood purges the sanctuary's uncleanness and the scapegoat purges the sins of the people. As Milgrom (1044) notes, now we have the big picture: "the causes of the sanctuary's impurities, all of Israel's sins, ritual and moral alike, of priests and laity alike."

In the ancient exorcism customs behind this chapter it may be that two goats were used, perhaps in the manner of the two birds used in Lev 14. Here Priestly writers have recast the second goat for *Azazel* as a dramatic reminder of the effects of sin. The scapegoat does not have to be killed, but it must be sent to *Azazel's* wilderness domain, a place of no return.

The special linen vestments may have been a reminder of the tradition that angels wore linen garments when in God's presence (see Ezek 9:2–3, 11). In Lev 16 the purification rites are extensive, and then bathing and more formal garments are needed for presiding at the *burnt offerings* in 16:24. As Aaron changes vestments and bathes before the next part of the ceremony (16:23–24), we should think of the linen robes as holy, not impure. In the same way, the bathing (apparently within the courtyard) need not indicate impurity, but rather it might br a way of honoring the boundaries of purity of the holy of holies, a way of having Aaron return to his more normal or less sacrosanct everyday state. Later, Herod's temple had a priests' bathing structure (not simply a set of curtains or a tent) in the southeast part of the outer courtyard.

We can assume that the high priest is never made unclean by officiating at purgation rituals. But the attendant becomes temporarily unclean when he leaves the camp (or Jerusalem) to take the scapegoat away. Those who incinerate the bull and the goat used in the purification offerings also have the same status, as did all those involved in preparing the ashes of the red heifer. None of these participants, some of whom may be priests, is as immune or especially holy as the high priest during these ceremonies.

The appendix or parallel passage in 16:29–34 is most likely from the Holiness tradition. The verb *deny* (*ynh*) in 16:29, 31 means *humbling* or *afflicting;* either man or God can be the one doing the afflicting. The verb by itself does not specify the mode, subject or object. The context must explain. *Fasting* might not have been the most appropriate or practical discipline for everyone, although most translators and readers would accept that broad image. The statement in 16:30 that all this *cleanses you* merges the images of purification and forgiveness. Strictly speaking, the rite cleanses the sanctuary or temple, but we can assume that the people's participation in this day through their self-abnegation aids in their being cleansed.

Commentators find it quite challenging to organize the various lunar, solar, agricultural, and liturgical calendar systems found in the Old Testament. The several sets of holy days in the seventh month, Tishri, are especially burdened with multiple traditions. This was the month after the harvests and prior to the rainy season.

The first of the month (23:24) may have inaugurated a period of praying for the coming rain. There is no clear biblical explanation for the current ceremonies of the same day, known as Rosh Hashanna, the new year festival. Older theories about possible ancient Jewish new year customs included the suggestion that the tenth of the month ended an extended period of celebration, and that an annual purification of the sanctuary was simply a part of getting the new year under way.

It is also possible that the original rites on the tenth of Tishri (23:27–32) were not as solemn as we now understand them from Lev 16. Scholars note that the system of Jubilees in Lev 25 begin on this same day, the tenth of Tishri. The fiftieth-year Jubilee is mentioned in Lev 25:9; real estate had to be deeded back to the original tribes (25:10–34) and indentured Hebrews were released from their obligations (25:35–55). Major nationwide realignments such as these may seem at odds with an annual penitential rite.

Later rabbis noted that the Day of Atonement was one of the two days each year when marriageable young women performed communal dances to encourage prospective husbands. Having events of this kind on this Day of Atonement each year is equally surprising.

In any case, Lev 16 focuses on purification and penance. From what we know of ancient Near Eastern ceremonies involving animals or birds used as scapegoats, they were only used in emergencies. Communal fasting was also quite unusual; it was thought of as a way to respond to a divine initiative or punishment. Jewish leaders could have linked such crises to the sins of the nation. The image of the king of Nineveh calling for fasting and repentance (Jon 3:7–9) is a good example of this notion. Obviously the prophets often did the same.

Milgrom offers evidence that this focus on penance in Lev 16 is old, certainly pre-exilic. Given the frequency of emergencies (drought, blight, disease in flocks or among the people, misfortunes of war, etc.), perhaps priests overused the rites for purifying the sanctuary and calling everyone to fasting and abstention from labor. With overuse, public apathy could have developed. Milgrom suggests that the later Holiness school of priests may have modified the custom and insisted that there be only one Day of Atonement each year. Then the focus on purification and penance could be more easily maintained. An effective annual penance ritual, properly prepared, could well contribute to the spiritual temper and morale of the community, as Yom Kippur still does today.

Question

54. Imagine yourself to be the high priest on this day. What emotions do you think you might feel during all this? Imagine yourself to be the one designated to take the scapegoat to the remote wilderness. What emotions do you think you might feel during all this?

Conclusion

Old Testament commentators often examine rituals from neighboring cultures, looking for commonalities and differences with Jewish thought. Usually the differences are more notable. Milgrom cites several Hittite scapegoat exorcisms used to drive away disease-bearing demons. These demons are controlled by deities who need to be placated. By contrast, Aaron is atoning for the sins of his people, not fighting demons. The references to Azazel are simply figures of speech, as noted earlier.

Leviticus 17:1—27:34

Section Thirteen

LEVITICUS 17:1–16

The final eleven chapters of Leviticus come from a later subdivision of the Priestly editors, commonly called the Holiness school (H). The average reader can catch some of the style, logic, and theology of this school, although the topics and laws seem to be piled up in what we would probably at first call a disorganized warehouse.

I think that as average readers (probably Christians or possibly Jewish people who are not veterans of rabbinic education) we may feel twice removed from all this material. The laws and codes are from almost three thousand years ago, and the rules for animal sacrifices are moot since there is no functioning temple now, nor should there be in the future.

Even so, perhaps we can try to think of ourselves as law students; specifically, we can try to learn what God wanted from his people (which somehow does include all of us).

One step in playing law students will be to consider some fairly specific verse-by-verse questions right now, before the usual introductory material. Keep some written notes to see how well your first impressions mesh with the rest of this entire section on Lev 17.

Questions

55. Contrast 17:1–4 with 17:5–7. Are they two equal parts of one speech or one law? Does the phrase *and say to them further* in 17:8 simply introduce the next paragraph, or does it shed any light on this question about the two equal parts of one speech?

56. What is the difference in content in 17:8–9, as compared to the first seven verses?

57. Is there any way that 17:10 stands alone?

58. Contrast 17:11–12 with 17:10. Are they two equal parts of one speech or one law?

59. What is different about 17:13, taken alone?

60. How does 17:14 supplement 17:13 or 17:10–13?

61. What is the difference in content in 17:15–16, as compared to the rest of the chapter?

62. Lev 17:1–7 is for all the people of Israel, but non-Jewish resident aliens are mentioned or included by implication in just about every remaining verse (17:8 [+9], 10, 12, 13, 15 [+16]). If we assume that these resident aliens are not in any way obligated to observe the rules of 17:1–7, why do they get mentioned so often in the rest of the chapter?

63. Do the mentions of lawbreakers being *cut off* (17:4, 9, 10, 14) and bearing their guilt (17:16) give any help to the reader?

Scholars note the Holiness school's preference for large and small chiasms (inverted sequences of topics) and some new vocabulary. In various contexts the key phrase *I am the LORD* could have the sense of *This is the declaration of the LORD* or *I, the LORD, have spoken*. In Holiness texts precise or concrete Priestly terms are often turned into metaphors, or are blurred or interchanged in other ways. Milgrom refers to H having a "cavalier disregard" for terms used consistently in P. At other places in H there is more emphasis on moral impurity (which demands deeper repentance) than on ritual impurity, the main focus of P.

Holiness editors put things in new ways at times. For them Israel is only a *tenant* (*ger*, same word means *resident alien*) on the land, which belongs to God; if they sin, they can be evicted.

Within these chapters the *resident aliens* could be considered the same as the *mixed crowd* of Exod 12:38. In later centuries the term refers to non-Jews allowed to live in the country for various reasons (descendants of conquered Canaanites, freed slaves, etc.). While they had some civil rights, most were day laborers or simple artisans; they had little chance to purchase land, since that was strongly controlled by tribal laws.

They were under religious restrictions, such as the proper disposal of animal blood mentioned in this chapter, and removing leaven along with everyone else during the Week of Unleavened Bread. They were not allowed to have polytheistic rites in public. Any of the alien men who wanted to celebrate the Passover meal had to be circumcised, and anyone who wanted to make other offerings at Israelite shrines had to meet the same standards of religious purity and cleanness.

Another example of fine-tuning is that, for H, God moves about the land, rather than remaining exclusively within the sanctuary. This can be seen in the blessings of 26:11–12, "I will place my dwelling in your midst, and I shall not abhor you. And I will walk among you, and will be your God, and you shall be my people."

The Hebrew word for *dwelling* here is actually *mishkan*, one of the main words for *tent* or *tabernacle*. Milgrom thinks a better translation would be *I will establish my presence in your midst*. This broadens the image to a metaphor. He cites Ezek 37:26–28 in support; there Ezekiel (using our passage from Leviticus) depicts God's *sanctuary* (*mqdsh*, *holy place*) among his people, and speaks of his *mishkan* being *over them* (NRSV has *with them*). Milgrom translates the phrase in Ezek 37:27 as *my presence shall rest over them*. He prefers to see this initiative by God as "an ethereal, spatially unbounded presence," and notes the later rabbinic way of speaking about God's presence, his *shekinah* (presence hidden within a bright light).

Lev 26:12 continues with God promising to *walk among you*. The verb for *walking* (*hlk*) is in a special form (reflexive) that usually means *walking about* or *walking to and fro*. It can easily imply spending time being with someone and sharing in intimate conversation.

Examples of the verb in this form in Ezek 19:6; 28:14; 2 Sam 7:6–7 demonstrate the basic meaning of *walking about* or *to and fro*. The last quotation in 2 Sam 7 will come up a few paragraphs below in connection with the local shrines.

The extended meaning of being with people and conversing intimately with them is best found in passages in Genesis that use this reflexive verb form. In Gen 3:8 God is described as *walking about* in the garden of Eden, where he normally conversed with Adam and Eve. In Gen 5:24 Enoch *walks* with God, and Noah does the same in 6:9. God tells Abraham to *walk before me* in 17:1, and Abraham speaks of *the LORD, before whom I walk* in 24:40. In 48:15 Jacob refers to Abraham and Isaac *walking before God.* All these Genesis examples help H to exhort Israelites to observe the commandments.

At times H will contradict legal points that are fairly clear in P (or in the other layers of tradition in the Pentateuch). One example of that will come up now in Lev 17:1–9.

Lev 17 starts off without any special introduction, leaving the reader with no idea that he or she is meeting a new school of thought. Milgrom calls Lev 17 a "bridge chapter," and reminds us that Lev 1 started off the same way, with instructions for specific sacrifices. We can divide the chapter into the following parts.

17:1–7   All butchering of cattle, sheep and goats for family consumption by Israelites is to take place at the tabernacle. Resident aliens are not required to observe this law; they may prepare meat at home. The writers assume that this law depicts not only the original camp ruled by Moses, but later village life when local shrines served the people, long before the centralization at the one great shrine in Jerusalem. This law recasts all such ordinary butchering as well-being offerings (17:5–6), with blood dashed against the altar, fat portions put into the fire on the altar, and a portion set aside for the local priest. The final verse offers a rationale for this new regulation: restricting butchering to the local shrines should help prevent idolatrous sacrifices to other gods, here disparagingly referred to as goat-demons.

17:8–9   In ancient times converting from one faith to another was not common, since most religions were tribal or national. Within Israel, resident aliens could be religiously affiliated (to use a modern term) by following specific Jewish customs. They were not forced to affiliate, but they were barred from the public worship of idols.

17:10–12   These verses serve as the axis of the entire chapter. The prohibition against eating blood with meat is paramount for all Israelites and resident aliens. Blood represents the life forces that God controls, and is used as the method of atonement (mentioned twice in 17:11). Milgrom prefers to use *ransom* instead of *atonement* in that verse, and he uses *ingesting* (blood) rather than *eating* (blood) in 17:10-14.

17:13-14 Clean wild animals and birds taken as game, and not destined for sacrifice, may be butchered at home as long as the blood is drained on the ground and covered with earth. Lev 17:14 echoes 17:12, but applies to all animals, not just those used at sacrifices.

17:15-16 These verses mention simple regulations regarding short periods of uncleanness for those who eat of animals which had died naturally or were killed by predators. Under these provisions, the eating of the meat is permissible.

Many devices assist the unity of this chapter. The three increasingly serious topics—(prohibitions) of having all herd animals destined for food offered as well-being sacrifices, avoiding any idolatry, and disposing of blood in the proper way—are followed by the two permissions about game animals and the use of herd animals that died naturally or from predation.

Lev 17:2 is addressed to everyone. This is done often in H. See 21:24, which recasts the introduction of priestly laws in 21:1, since Moses spoke to everyone. See also 22:17-25, where everyone is told about not using blemished animals for sacrifices. These fine points could have been left up to the priests, but H insists that everyone had been told about them. Such information could even help laymen watch to see that the priests performed their duties correctly.

Note the frequent use of the first person in 17:10-12, 14. H uses this direct style often. In 17:10 the phrase *I will set my face against* is quite anthropomorphic. See Lev 20:3, 6; Ezek 14:8 for the same phrase. Priestly editors avoided graphic vocabulary of this sort. The other remark in Lev 17:10, *I will cut that person off*, is a rare first-person form; usually the sinner is *cut off* (passive form, not identifying the doer of the action). See 20:3, 5, 6 for the same phrase.

Leviticus 17:1—27:34

Some words are repeated often for effect. *Blood* (*dam*) is used ten times in 17:10-14, and once in 17:4, where it means *bloodguilt* (NRSV has *guilty of bloodshed*).

Another device used by authors depicting speeches is the *aside*, some phrase or sentence spoken to the audience or perhaps to a few participants in the scene. One could consider the explanations in 17:5-7, 11-12, 14 as asides, spoken to Moses to help him understand what is going on. The phrases in 17:8, *and say to them further*, and in 17:12 and 14, *I have said to the people of Israel*, help identify the asides. Most modern readers ignore this matter of asides, since we get to read all of those six verses. Still, the asides may have been used to emphasize that the custom of preparing meat at home has now been changed, or that the blood regulations are very, very important, or that there has been some recent laxness regarding idolatry.

The heart of the asides is found in 17:11. The phrase *I have given it to you for making atonement* refers to the Israelites alone, since the sentence next mentions the altar. We can also see that 17:11 is a counterbalance to the statements in 17:3-5. There the people and priests offer the well-being sacrifices with the dashing of the blood and the burning of the fat portions; here, in the larger sense, God has given it (the blood of the well-being sacrifices) to them so that they may make atonement. The only offering where one eats the meat (after removing the blood) is in fact the well-being offering.

The *atonement* or *ransom for your lives* in 17:11 refers back to the *bloodshed* or *bloodguilt* in 17:4. This is all part of the ethic of life based on Gen 9:1-8, where God made the concession for humanity to take animals for their meat, while respecting the seriousness of the necessary killing. The same ethic is behind the division of clean and unclean animals for sacrifice and for the table. As Milgrom notes, the proper disposal of the blood of well-being sacrifices (or the blood of animals butchered by resident aliens) atones for the actual killing of the animal.

The mention of *the life of every creature* and *the blood of any creature* in 17:14 is meant to cover the different cases of the resident alien and the Israelite. Both must properly dispose of the blood of the animals they eat, but the Israelite alone is obligated to offer herd animals as well-being sacrifices. To put it another way, the Israelite has to undertake more complex steps for ransom or atonement, while the resident alien may achieve that same ransom or atonement much more easily.

The regulations in Lev 17:15–16 are more lenient than we find in Exod 22:31 and Deut 14:21. For H the unintended death of any herd animal represents lost income; any honorable use of the hide, meat, or fat could make the financial loss less burdensome.

Conclusion

Milgrom deals with two historical questions at this point: the importance of local shrines and the type of idolatry represented by the *goat-demons*. First, he argues that the H material is mainly from the eighth century BCE (a date much earlier than that accepted by some other scholars). During this period many local shrines remained open, even though David and Solomon had set up the central shrine in Jerusalem. So the H notion that Israelites should present all meat as well-being offerings at local shrines would have been possible, but only for the period of time before the local shrines were completely discontinued.

Some argue that the slaughtering of meat for a family would have only occurred a few times each year. Milgrom takes the opposite position, noting that most young male herd animals were quite expendable. Most were not needed for breeding, nor did they produce the milk for the young or for dairy products.

Many local shrines are mentioned in the Old Testament: Beer-sheba, Bethel, Gilgal, Shechem, Shilo, and others. The ark at different times was kept at Bethel, Gilgal, or Shilo. In 2 Sam 7:6 God says to Nathan, "I have not lived in a house since the day I brought up the people of Israel from Egypt to this day, but I have been moving about in a tent and a tabernacle." So we have a hint of multiple sanctuaries sharing the ark. A few scholars go so far as to speculate that there might even have been more than one version of the ark itself.

Num 5:3 speaks of lepers staying outside *the camps* so as not to defile the LORD's sanctuary. This may be another hint about multiple shrines, even though many translators simply put *camp* in the singular. In Lev 26:31 God speaks of making *your sanctuaries desolate*. Here the noun is clearly in the plural.

Secondly, Milgrom calls attention to the sort of idolatry that H criticizes. The references to sacrifice *in the open field* in Lev 17:5 and to the *goat-demons* in 17:7 point to troubling rituals involving the gods of the underworld and of death. Other hints at *augury, witchcraft, gashing flesh for the dead, mediums,* and *wizards* in 19:26–31 seem to support this anxiety about the gods of the underworld.

In 1 Sam 14:31–35 Saul reprimanded his troops for improperly slaughtering some sheep and oxen to eat at the end of a battle. The first verse says the men slaughtered the animals *on the ground* and *ate them with the blood.* This last phrase is mentioned two more times in 14:33–34. Saul had the men resume the slaughtering on a large stone placed near where he was. The final verse mentions that Saul built an altar to the LORD, although it is not clear that the altar was made from the large stone just mentioned.

Milgrom challenges some of the translation. He argues for slaughtering the animals *facing the ground* in 1 Sam 14:31, and for the three instances of *with the blood* he prefers reading *over the blood*. Both of his challenges have more than average merit. The augury and witchcraft mentioned in Lev 19:26 is linked with the same phrase about eating *over the blood*.

Milgrom assembles evidence that in many ancient cultures the gods of the underworld were in charge of séances with the dead and of ancestor worship. These serious superstitions often involved animal blood being poured into a trench or pit outdoors or within a cavern or other underground site. The blood was thought to attract underworld spirits and souls of the dead. Slaughtering the animal as it was forced to *face the ground* was another symbolic procedure for the same purpose of contacting the forces of the underworld.

So Saul had his men use a stone instead of a trench or pit in the ground, and all the blood was properly drained and buried following God's instructions, not those of underworld gods. If Saul was merely policing non-sacrificial slaughter, then the stone was not considered an altar and the slaughter was not part of a well-being ritual.

The goat-demons could well have been part of local polytheistic belief systems about the underworld and ancestor worship. Images in Isa 13:21; 34:14 and Deut 32:17 seem to support this theory. Milgrom notes that perhaps the *Azazel* mentioned in Lev 16 had been one of those goat-demons or satyrs. There is even the possibility that the H school was registering a subtle criticism about the scapegoat component of the rites for the Day of Atonement. They may have felt that the use of the scapegoat kept some superstitions alive, even though that was not the intention.

Section Thirteen

Looking ahead to the rest of Leviticus, Milgrom admires the H traditions about ethics and social justice, and tries to put the requirement for bringing all the animals for well-being sacrifices within that broader context. Milgrom (1507) admits that the requirement may have been "so idealistic as to be beyond realization," but credits the H school for being "sensitively aware of the problems besetting their fellow Israelites outside the sanctuary precincts, problems for which they propose far-reaching remedies and a comprehensive blueprint for achieving an ideal society."

Milgrom ends this section with a clear overview of some of the variations between P and H, and mentions that the Deuteronomists (D) later on approved of the closing of all local shrines in favor of Jerusalem. So in Deuteronomy permission is again granted to all to butcher their nonsacrificial animals at home, since it would be impossible to bring the meat back home all the way from Jerusalem.

Section Fourteen

LEVITICUS 18:1–30

For this chapter we will consider four questions at the outset, rather than at the usual position later on.

Questions

64. Consider 18:1–5 and 18:24–30 by themselves. They clearly introduce and conclude a set of laws and warnings, but how do they help the reader get into the right frame of mind?

65. Looking at 18:6–18 at one initial glance, how do the editors present the main subject? As a reader, do you have any initial reactions to the way this passage is presented?

66. Looking at 18:19–23 at one initial glance, how does this passage relate to 18:6–18?

67. Why is Lev 18 so lengthy? The authors could have combined parts of God's speeches and condensed the prohibitions and so shortened the chapter by a third or a half.

This chapter contains a complicated list of prohibitions, including incest and relationships with in-laws, etc. The opening (18:1–5) and closing sections (18:24–30) illustrate some clear points of the theology of H. The several personal statements by God himself (*I am the LORD* [4x] *... the land of Canaan, to which I am bringing you ... my ordinances, my statutes ... the nations I am casting out ... I punished it for its iniquity ... my charge*) add to the solemnity of the whole, and highlight God as the personal lawgiver.

The condemnation of Egyptian and Canaanite sexual customs is stereotypical. In fact some degrees of prohibition of marriage with in-laws and distant cousins still vary from one culture to another. Some ancient royal families, where the rulers were considered semi-divine, had special systems for themselves. Note the pharaonic line, where some levels of incest between the pharaoh and his sisters were customary. But ordinary Egyptians and Canaanites lived family lives fairly similar to the Israelites, as far as we can tell. Painting the other nations as steeped in sin may have been a graphic way of reminding Israelites of how easy it is to start down that slippery slope.

In 18:5 obeying God's statutes and ordinances supports life itself. While the phrase *one shall live* points to each individual, the life of the community will also benefit from the observance of these moral customs. All these laws prohibit either certain formal attempts at marriage or consensual or forced intercourse.

Lev 18 can be subdivided as follows:

18:1–5 Introduction

18:6–16 Sexual relations with immediate family and in-laws

18:17–18 Additional cases

18:19–23 Other prohibitions

18:24–30 Conclusion

Within the main block of prohibitions, addressed to an individual Israelite man, the following laws are mentioned. Remember that polygamy and divorce (initiated by the husband) were allowed, and widows were free to decide to remarry or not. The rabbinic understanding is that an individual Israelite woman would be subject to many (but not all) of the same standards as the men, simply by reading *sister* for *brother*, *daughter* for *son*, etc. A rough outline of the prohibitions will be offered here, with additional verse-by-verse comments following.

You may not marry:

18:6 Anyone near of kin (*nshr bshrw*, literally *flesh of one's body*, i.e., immediate blood relative). Commentators assume that this phrase covers some of the cases not mentioned in detail in the rest of the chapter (e.g., your own grandparents). See 21:2–3 for a short list of immediate family, including sisters who have never married. In 25:49 some immediate family are urged to assist a poor relative with loans.

18:7	Your own mother
18:8	Any stepmother (any other wife of your father)
18:9	Any half-sister (e.g., from your mother by any other spouse, raised in your father's household)
18:10	Any granddaughter of yours
18:11	Any foster sister informally adopted into your father's clan
18:12	Any paternal aunt (full sister of your father)
18:13	Any maternal aunt (full sister of your mother)
18:14	Any wife of your father's full brother (your paternal uncle)
18:15	Any daughter-in-law
18:16	Any sister-in-law

Since we have two lists regarding incest and other sexual wrongdoings in Leviticus (18:6–23; 20:10–21) and other lists elsewhere in the Old Testament, some scholars suggest that these problems may have been widespread at times.

Casting the laws in the second-person singular (*thy mother, thy father...*) helps make the laws more personal and urgent.

Milgrom notes that the basic Israelite family unit was the *father's house*—about fifty to one hundred people, covering three to five generations, living in close proximity. Closer groups of kin (about twenty, usually) lived in small single-family houses around a common courtyard. When the *father's house* grew too large, younger sons might break off to start a new *father's house*, but family bonds would still unite them into a larger *house of the fathers*. We usually call these larger units *clans*. Heads of houses and of clans had judicial powers, along the lines that the *paterfamilias* had in Roman culture.

The frequent mentions that *I am the LORD* in chapters with prohibitions like these certainly raise the image of God as judge and jury. He will make sure punishment comes, but a paterfamilias would also be obligated to challenge family members when they were involved in forbidden relationships. As Milgrom notes, the blood relatives in 18:6–16 live in the family compound and are under the control of the paterfamilias. The forbidden liaisons may be consensual, and, even if discovered, there is no one to bring the paterfamilias to act justly, except God himself.

The Hebrew word order in 18:3–4 emphasizes the deeds of others and the laws of God, by putting these ahead of the verbs: *. . . the deeds of Egypt you shall not do; . . . the deeds of Canaan you shall not do; my judgments you shall do and my laws you shall keep.*

At the end of 18:5 we switch to the third-person *one shall live* instead of the expected *you shall live*. It is possible that the *one* spoken of could be an Israelite or a resident alien. The aliens will be mentioned in 18:26, but they must logically be included under all these prohibitions.

Before going into further detail about individual verses, we could speculate as to the grand purpose of the entire list. On one level these rules can promote peace within a large household, but, as Milgrom notes, the main goal could be procreation and child rearing within an ordered patriarchal structure. Thus 18:6–18, 20 point to offspring that would be destructive of family, and 18:19, 21–23 point to no offspring at all. Using shaming words such as *perversion, abomination,* and *depravity* can be very effective warnings. Some Asian cultures still have the internal social unity for standards of shame to affect the conduct of most of their citizens.

18:6

The plural verb form in 18:6 *none of you shall approach to uncover* serves as a transition from the plurals of 18:1–5 to all the singular verb forms in 18:7–23. *None of you* could also include the resident alien.

The Hebrew phrase for *anyone near of kin* is *any flesh of his body*, meaning *bloodline*. The Hebrew is a redundant or superlative idiom, meant to place strong emphasis on these relatives. To *approach* (*qrb*) to *uncover* (*glh*) *nakedness* (*yrwh*) may seem to be a very indirect euphemism, but there is no biblical Hebrew word for *genitals*. *Uncovering nakedness* is another superlative or redundant phrase used for emphasis.

Milgrom, citing J. R. Ziskind, points to the goal of 18:6.

[Its author] intended these prohibitions to be absolute, to transcend the laws of rape, seduction and adultery and to be lifelong, i.e., from the time that the relationship was established by either birth or marriage, and not to end with death or divorce.... . Accordingly, a man would now be forbidden to have sex with his stepmother not only in his father's lifetime but after his father died. He was also barred from sex with his daughter-in-law and sister-in-law on the death of his son or brother (hence no levirate).... Women could no longer be handed around to other men in the family as wives and concubines. A widow could now marry anyone she wished outside the family or could be free not to remarry at all.... The rules forbidding a man to marry a woman and then to marry or make a concubine of her mother, daughter or sister prevented the unseemliness of a man moving about from one member of a woman's family to another, and thus ended an abuse in the practice of polygamy.... H did not wish any dilution of affection to take place among sisters or between mother and daughter by reason of a circumstance in which these women were forced to compete for the attention of the same man. (1534–35)

Milgrom (1535) cites a paragraph from Maimonides, one of Judaism's finest medieval commentators, that also points to the same potential imbalances of power within ancient households.

All illicit unions with females have one thing in common: namely, that in the majority of cases these females are constantly in the company of the male in his house and that they are easy of access for him and can easily be controlled by him—there being no difficulty in making them come to his presence; and no judge could blame the male for their being with him. Consequently if the status of the woman with whom union is illicit were that of any unmarried woman, I mean to say that if it were possible and that the prohibition with regard to them were only due to their not being the man's wives, most people would have constantly succumbed and fornicated with them. (*Guide* 3.49)

18:7

The Hebrew of 18:7 starts out with *The nakedness of your father and (=that is) the nakedness of your mother not shall you uncover*. Here *the father's nakedness* might be a phrase describing his jurisdiction or responsibility over the nakedness of his wife. This could apply also in verses 8b (*the nakedness of your father*), 10 (*your own nakedness*), 14 (*the nakedness of your father's brother*), and 16b (*it is your brother's nakedness*).

Another guess is that the *nakedness of your father* in 18:7-8 is a phrase that was added by H to an older list of offenses, and that here it means that having sex with one's mother is tantamount to having sex with one's father. See verses 10 (*your nakedness, i.e., your own granddaughters'*), 12 (*she is your father's flesh*), and 16 (*it is your brother's nakedness*).

18:8

This refers to any stepmother, if the father had a second wife or several wives or concubines. It is not clear whether the addressee's own mother is still alive, nor do we know the current age of the addressee; were he an adult, he might have been tempted. Given the young age at which women married then, a son in his late teens might become interested in a stepmother nearly his age. Milgrom argues that this prohibition holds even if the addressee's father, the husband of the stepmother in question, has died.

18: 9, 11

At first it seems that the subject in 18:9 is one's sister or half-sister. The reference to *born at home or born abroad* is odd. It might refer to a very young daughter of a widowed or divorced stepmother who then married the addressee's father, and now that very young daughter has come of age. Milgrom argues that the word *mwldt* is not a verb form meaning to *be born*, but a related noun that refers to a *clan*. Then the Hebrew reference to the *clan at home* or the *clan outside* (*abroad*) means *the father's clan* or *someone else's clan*. See Gen 12:1; 24:4 and Num 10:30 for uses of this related noun; in all three cases the NRSV has *kindred*, but the context could certainly refer to *clan*. In either case, the child was raised by the father of the addressee, and so has certain rights.

The possible use of the word *clan* comes up again in 18:11. The subject is foster sisters, any of your father's other wives' daughters raised but not sired by him. The phrase *begotten by your father* comes from the Septuagint. The Hebrew again has the word *mwldt*, which could mean *of your father's clan*. The woman, although not related directly to the addressee, is protected by the paternal clan customs. Had she been of the mother's clan, she would be an eligible bride for the addressee.

18:10

Obviously having sexual relations with one's own granddaughter is incest. Calling this *your own nakedness* means that your granddaughter is within your own jurisdiction or responsibility as the paterfamilias until she marries.

18:12–14

In these verses aunts by blood are covered, even though aunts usually did not live in the compound. Rabbis allowed for the opposite case: that uncles by blood could marry nieces.

In 18:14 we have a prohibition covering an aunt by marriage, a wife of the father's brother. The father's brother (*dod*) was his most important male relative, and his wife (*doda*) had a special status. The brother of someone's mother had less standing in these family hierarchies.

18:15–16

The law includes any daughter-in-law (*klh*), even if now divorced or widowed. The sister-in-law mentioned in 18:16 could be the wife of a younger brother who still lives at home. If this law holds even after the brother's death, it contradicts the older levirate custom mentioned in Deut 25:5–9.

18:17

To understand this case, let us think of a woman (A), her daughter (B), and her granddaughter (C), the daughter of B or a son (X), otherwise unidentified. The two women A and B, both living, are not related to the addressee at all. The phrase *you shall not take to uncover* could refer to marriage rather than simply sexual activity. One could think of an addressee being about forty-five, illicitly involved with A, but getting serious with fifteen-year-old granddaughter C, not related to him. The NRSV has the warning *they are your flesh*, a variant text that is confusing since they are not blood relatives of the addressee. The Hebrew has *they are her flesh*, referring to woman A, which is a correct designation. Milgrom notes that any relationships of the man with B or C are prohibited, even if there is consent to a ménage à trois.

18:18

The next three verses deal with different topics. Lev 18:18 is quite clear: a man cannot marry the first and second of two living sisters; the second will surely *be in rivalry* (*zrr*) with the first. In 1 Sam 1:6 the related noun *zrh* is used for a *rival wife*. This prohibition was only for the lifetime of the first sister; after her death a marriage would be allowed. In some cultures marrying the second sister at that point was an honorable choice, especially if she could help raise minor children from the first wife.

18:19

Note that H considers this blood taboo inexpiable, and that it affects the whole land.

18:20

This rule forbids adultery with a wife of a *kinsman* (*ym*). The word *ym* means distant relatives of any sort, perhaps on the father's side. Milgrom translates it as a *neighbor's* wife. The problem is not simply the betraying of a husband; questions of paternity lay behind property and inheritance disputes as well.

The adultery defiles both parties, as well as the land. In that sense adultery is seen as a religious offense, not simply a civil offense that could be pardoned by some sort of fine.

18:21

In the midst of all these prohibitions we might be surprised by the topic of child sacrifices to *Molek* (*Molech*). The Canaanites are described as worshipers of Molek, the chief god of the underworld and enabler of contact with ancestors. The sacrifice of infants was at times part of this terribly superstitious system.

The prohibition here is against Israelites who had succumbed to some of these ways of placating the forces of the underworld. Milgrom notes that perhaps infant grandchildren would have been at risk if a paterfamilias was tempted to offer a sacrifice.

In Ezek 16:20–21; 23:37–39; Deut 12:29–31; 18:9–12; and 2 Kgs 23:10 we have clear references to these sacrifices, identified in 2 Kgs 23 as taking place at Topheth, in the valley of Ben-hinnom, which is the ravine or gully below the Temple Mount in Jerusalem. The reference in Ezek 23 is especially graphic.

Milgrom examines various forms of the name *Molek/Molech*. It may be a participle from a common verb, meaning *he who rules*, or it may be a proper name such as *Malik*, based on the same verb. This Canaanite god was served with sporadic and limited infant sacrifices. For the H editors, the Canaanite tolerance of incest and their service of Molek had both contributed to the land vomiting them out.

It was a sorry enough set of circumstances that some Israelites picked up some of these superstitions. Even worse, they seem to have found this compatible with a basic allegiance to Yahweh. Zeph 1:4–5 gives examples of the people following Yahweh and other gods at the same time. Jeremiah rails against these human sacrifices, noting that God never commanded such sacrifices and indeed had never even given that a thought at all (see Jer 7:31; 19:5; 32:35). The passages in Jeremiah have an argumentative tone to them, clearly an attempt to deny a popular Israelite notion that service to Molek was acceptable.

Milgrom argues that ordinary Israelites were not fusing Yahweh and Molek into one divinity, but rather dealing with each as the chief god in his own realm. They thought of Yahweh as the chief god of the nation, a high god such as the astral deities of creation and sun and moon, etc. Molek then was a high deputy serving under Yahweh, with his own control of the realm of the underworld and access to ancestors. This is of course a form of dualism, the polytheistic notion that the explanation for evil and suffering is that there are gods of good and gods of evil.

In an earlier monograph, Alberto Green noted that sacrifices to Molek in the eight and seventh centuries BCE were universally condemned in the Old Testament, but may have persisted "during national emergencies caused by external pressures and wars" (187). In his broader conclusions about many types of human sacrifice in the ancient Near East, Green noted:

> The evidence also reveals certain poignant factors about the behavior of ancient man. What intermittent indications of human sacrifice exist prove that two major exercises of political power, namely law and war, always involved the death of persons. Since power in the ancient world was legitimized by the gods, both had to have legitimization. The law which sanctioned the death of individuals was, therefore, viewed as a "rite" required by deity. War could not be merely secular; it was religious. . . . All evidence examined points to "human sacrifice" during times of political or domestic crisis. On such occasions the context in which the ritual occurs is usually that of a degenerate civilization attempting to find solutions to problems based on a misunderstanding of the past. (202)

Green's remarks help us to see that sometimes the contact sought with ancestors may well have been for the purpose of getting answers about battles and wartime alliances.

I give extra space to this troubling issue of infant sacrifice to remind us of the long struggle within Israel over polytheism and the dark fears about drought, disease, war, and death that led to many unhealthy superstitions. Throughout the Bible we find many harsh references to gods and goddesses (Baals, Asherahs, queens of moon or heavens, rain gods, the satan [accusing angel] and the like). The biblical references provide us with realistic evidence of some of this struggle, and in so doing serve us better than any whitewashing process could have done.

At another point, Milgrom examines the issue of firstborn males. Some commentators speculate about ancient sacrifices of these sons to Yahweh or to Molek or to other gods. In Num 18:15–19 the firstborn of cattle are to be offered in sacrifice, and firstborn sons are to be redeemed for a set price. One theory is that the redemption stands for what was originally a sacrifice, or, more likely, for a period of service at a local shrine. Milgrom disputes the evidence for this theory of frequent human sacrifice and concludes, "in sum, there is no evidence that the firstborn, except in crisis situations (e.g., 2 Kgs 3:27), were sacrificed; there is no indication that Israel's God ever demanded or even sanctioned this practice (except in popular belief); and there is no connection between the firstborn and the Molek" (1590).

18:22

This verse condemns homosexual relations, calling them an *abomination* (*tyb*). This same term of shame will be repeated in 18:26, 27, 29, 30, where it refers to the entire chapter, with all its sexual activities, and the sacrifices to Molek as well. Lev 18:22 and its parallels allow of no exceptions.

The reasons for the absolute ban of homosexuality in the Old Testament are not spelled out. In Lev 18 it is listed with offenses that defile the land, and so indicates the worry that someday Israel might be vomited out of its own place. Another simple guess is that since no children can come of such unions they thus would bring no benefit to a small nation. One could say that 18:22 is simply one of a list of prohibitions meant to promote stable family life wherein children may thrive.

I think it is fair to say that 18:22 by itself does not invite much discussion, nor shed much light on the current changes in our society's comprehension of homosexuality. Milgrom suggests that we could analyze 18:22 to mean "do not have sex with a male with whose widow sex is forbidden." But even that possible nuance is not of much help to us.

Lev 18:22 is a very brief statement within a list of prohibited actions. But the list itself presumes and supports a corporate spirituality very unlike our own. We tend to think of ourselves as individuals first, even in our relationships with God. We don't think of the land vomiting all of us out; rather God should target only those individuals who have done serious wrongs. In order to appreciate Old Testament corporate thinking we need to realize the limitations of our own strongly individualistic framework or outlook on the meaning of life.

Further, the marriage prohibitions involving blood relatives and in-laws, as well as the prohibitions against horrifying sacrifices to Molek, hint at the extent of those internal problems within Israelite society. The prohibitions in Leviticus did not make these problems go away. So too, issues surrounding homosexuality did not go away because of 18:22.

The prohibitions placed responsibilities on family leaders, such as the paterfamilias, but each family leader had to be able to confront family members heading in the wrong direction. Each family leader, man or woman, also had to lead by good example. This was not always the case.

18:24–30

In the closing section the sexual sins of the previous *nations* (*goiim*, which could also mean *peoples* or *tribes* rather than a political state with international standing) have defiled those people and their land. The defiled land itself *vomits out* (*qya*) those who have defiled it. This vomiting is described as virtually an automatic act of nature. Individuals who defile are *cut off* (18:28), and the land in some way loses its ability to sustain life and so drives away those peoples or tribes. Israel will be subject to the same law of nature, as we read in 18:28–29, "otherwise the land will vomit *you* out for defiling it, as it vomited out the *nation that was before you*. For *whoever* commits any of these abominations shall be cut off from *their people*."

The H editors do not spell out the breaking point, the point at which expulsion will be inevitable, but it is an important question for any society to ponder.

Lev 18:26 mentions the *resident alien* (*ger*) for the first time. They are included since these sexual violations and child sacrifices defile the land no matter who brings them about.

Conclusion

There seems to be no prohibition in Lev 18 nor elsewhere in the Old Testament against the marriage of first cousins. This may even have been a preferred arrangement with regard to keeping property within a clan, and is still a custom in some parts of the world with strong codes about clan and tribal property and inheritance.

Milgrom also notes that in Lev 18 intermarriage with non-Israelites is not mentioned. Perhaps this is an indicator of the pre-exilic age of the P and H traditions. When Israel had more control of their own land, intermarriages usually involved the new wife following Jewish customs. At other points in the history of Israel any intermarriage was seen as a disaster for the nation.

Section Fifteen

LEVITICUS 19:1–37

Questions

I think it is important for readers to scan all of Lev 19 at one sitting at the outset. A group could have someone read all of it aloud. I recommend doing this again, and ending with two or three repetitions of 19:2, before trying to answer question 76.

68. Assuming that 19:5–8 might have meant more to the original audience than it does to us, how is 19:3–8 related to 19:2?

69. If you take 19:3–8 and 19:11–12 as serious guidelines, how or why does it make sense to sandwich 19:9–10 in between?

70. Taking 19:11–16 as one unit for a moment, how can you turn all the cases of *you shall not* into a cohesive, positive goal?

71. How does 19:17–18 serve in relation to 19:3–16?

72. Why does the author consider reproving one's neighbor (19:17) as part of the cohesive, positive goal mentioned in question 70?

73. Clearly, 19:19 and 19:23–25 refer to customs understood by the original audiences. How odd is 19:20–22 compared to those other verses and, indeed, to the rest of the chapter? How do you think the man who had to bring the guilt offering felt during all this?

74. Lev 19:26–31 touches on very serious sins—much more serious than the worries about garments made of two different materials, or about when to eat the fruit of young orchard trees, and apparently more widespread than the occasional case of the designated

slave woman. What would happen if everyone ignored the religious and social norms being upheld in 19:26–31?

75. Note parallels between 19:18 and 19:34. Taking 19:33–37 as an appendix and a final conclusion to the chapter, how do these five verses contribute to the whole?

76. Think of the impact of the entirety of Lev 19; read it aloud (even if you are home alone) and repeat 19:2 two or three times at the end. How would you describe the main goal of what God wants his people to learn in this chapter?

Lev 19 touches on dozens of topics. The editors used the *I am the LORD* formula as a way to end many of the paragraphs. In a few cases a new paragraph begins simply because the subject matter changes at that point. Milgrom divides the chapter this way, with these subtitles.

19:1–2	Introduction
19:3	Revere parents and keep the Sabbath
19:4	Worship of other gods and images of Israel's God
19:5–8	The well-being offering
19:9–10	Horticultural holiness and required gifts to poor and aliens
19:11–13	Deeds
19:14	Exploitation of the helpless
19:15–16	Injustice and indifference
19:17–18	Reproof and love
19:19	Mixtures
19:20–22	The betrothed slave-woman
19:23–25	Horticultural holiness (continued)
19:26–28	Eschewing death and the dead
19:29	Prostitution, cultic or secular?
19:30	Sabbath and sanctuary
19:31	Consulting the dead

19:32	Respect for elders
19:33–34	The resident alien
19:35–36a	Business ethics
19:36b–37	Closing exhortation

We might be inclined to unite 19:13 and 19:14 into one paragraph because there is no special formula (such as *I am the LORD*) at the end of 19:13. The same is true for uniting 19:29 and 19:30. Special formulas are also missing at the end of 19:8, 19, 22. But in all these cases the subject changes in the next verse. Milgrom notes that in three of these five verses (19:8, 22, 29) the speech is in the third person rather than in the second, so a following direct statement such as *I am the LORD* would be awkward in style. For the sake of simplicity, we will use Milgrom's subdivisions of the chapter.

Milgrom takes 19:3-10 to be religious duties and 19:11-18 as ethical duties. The following group of verses, 19:19-29, is a miscellany, followed by what might have been the original ending of the chapter, 19:30-32. Then 19:33-36a could be taken as an appendix, preceding the closing exhortation in 19:36b-37. While these broad categorizations may be helpful, it does seem that much of the chapter touches on ethics.

The key verse of the entire chapter is 19:2. We are called upon to be holy because our God is holy. As Milgrom (1596) remarks, each and every topic that follows is "to set the people of Israel on the road to holiness." Holiness is open to all who will observe the religious prohibitions and fulfill the ethical ideals laid out. These various guidelines represent a "quality of holiness" in God, which his people should follow and perform.

In other parts of the Bible God's otherness is emphasized. God is intrinsically other; he *separates himself from* any sort of evil or injustice. But in promoting justice, forgiveness, and love, God, so to speak, *separates himself to* us; he works with us and does not simply wait within an elaborate sanctuary for worshipers to come in procession.

As Milgrom notes,

> For H, the God of the covenant is demanding more than obedience to his commandments (v. 37). He is also stating the rationale or, rather, the goal, the end product of the commandments. Obedience produces godliness, a quality encapsulated in the word *qadosh*, 'holy.' Just as the priests, who are innately holy, are qualified to enter into God's presence . . . , so Israel, in following

all YHWH's commandments, will attain holiness (v. 2), thereby also qualifying for perpetual admission into the presence—that is, the providence and protection—of God. (1606)

Moses is to repeat these directives to *all the congregation* (*kol adah*) of the people of Israel. This is a very comprehensive term, here meaning all the men, women, and children of the nation. It is found just this one time in Leviticus. The same introductory phrase is used in Exod 12:3 (for the main Passover regulations) and 35:1 (for gathering the materials for the Tabernacle), and in Num 1:2; 26:2 (for taking a census).

19:3

As 19:3 cites two of the Ten Commandments, we can see that the two chosen represent ethics (revering parents) and religious law (keeping the Sabbath). We could take this verse to signal the equal importance of both domains. In fact the mention of parents first and Sabbath second could be a deliberate attention-getter, as it reverses the order found in Exod 20.

The closing phrase, *I am the LORD your God*, can be taken two ways in context. It reminds us of the divine author of the commandments, and it also hints that serious punishments can follow disobedience.

19:4

The opening verb in 19:4, *do not turn* (*pnh*), means *do not seek help*, as we can see in 19:31, "*Do not turn to* (*pnh*) mediums or wizards; *do not seek* (*bqsh*) them out."

In 19:4 the term for *idols* (*alil*) is a negative and ridiculing one. The *cast images* might refer to images of God himself. The verse is obviously a reworking of the first two commandments.

19:5–8

One might wonder why the full details about when to eat the meat of a well-being sacrifice should appear in this chapter, and at such length. After all, we just reviewed the first four commandments in two short verses!

The original passage about well-being sacrifices in 7:16–18 has been modified slightly in Lev 19. The time span for eating the meat may be somewhat shorter in Lev 19, but more importantly, a reason is spelled out for not keeping the meat too long. In 19:5 you must *offer it in such a way that it is acceptable on your behalf*. This is specified in 9:8, since those who keep the meat too long *profane what is holy to the LORD*.

Keeping the meat too long is a health risk, although those who prepare the meat might feel that they can safely get one more meal out of what remains. But at this risky stage the meat left so long becomes too questionable as part of a holy sacrifice. If it now resembles anything other than the forces of life, it cannot be used. If the remains come to profane the sacrifice, the entire event is invalidated, and those who partook of any of it have now been defiled.

As Milgrom points out, the well-being sacrifice is the only sacrifice returned to the offerer for his own use; it is holy and must be treated carefully. Otherwise desecration will cancel whatever holiness is achieved in observing the other guidelines in this chapter. So the topic is not a peripheral fine point; the eating of a well-being animal is a direct participation in a sacrifice made holy at a shrine, and then brought to one's home, where it remains holy and must be handled with the utmost care.

19:9–10

The mention of providing gleanings from field or vineyard could be a bridge passage from the religious regulations in 19:3–8 to the ethical topics in 19:11–18. The authors assume we understand God's concern for the poor. There are no stipulations here about who is allowed to come to glean; even some resident aliens would be needy. There is also no advice on how much produce to leave behind for the gleaners. Ancient rabbis suggested a minimum of one-sixtieth of the crop.

19:11–13

Taking 19:11–13 as matters of justice, we are reminded of the passage in 6:1–7, which speaks of full restitution (plus one fifth extra) and the offering of a ram as a sin offering. The passage in Lev 19 is more comprehensive in vocabulary and style. Here the lies and false oaths may not have yet been confessed, but God is keeping track. The rationale for God's displeasure is the statement in 19:12 that *swearing falsely by my name* is *profaning the name of your God*. As Milgrom (1633) notes, these false oaths are sinful "against YHWH by preventing his holy presence from residing among Israel.... It is only when Israel is striving for a life of holiness, as encapsulated by the commandments of this chapter, that YHWH's otherness can be sustained on earth."

We noted earlier that the well-being sacrifice is the only sacrifice left to the care of the offerer. In another sense, the proper use of God's name is also the responsibility of each believer. If one uses the name falsely to promote an injustice, other techniques to achieve holiness are pointless.

The *laborer* (*skir*) mentioned in Lev 19:13 could be an Israelite or a resident alien. Deut 24:10–21 speaks of many opportunities for social justice. Laborers are mentioned in Deut 24:14–15: "You shall not withhold the wages of poor and needy laborers, whether Israelites or aliens who reside in your land in one of your towns. You shall pay them their wages daily before sunset, because they are poor and their livelihood depends on them."

19:14

The phrase *you shall not revile* (*qll*) often refers to *cursing*, but in this context we should broaden it to indicate any kind of *abuse* or *disrespect*, not only for deaf and blind persons but for all the weak and helpless who are God's special concern.

The remark that *you shall fear* (*ira*) *your God* is the right translation of this verb in this context. In many other situations having a *fear* (*irah*) *of the LORD* is best translated as having *awe*, which is a positive concept. The phrase will appear again in 19:32 with regard to the elderly, and at several points in Lev 25, which we shall examine later.

19:15–16

In court cases, or in judgments made make in business or personal relationships, one should not *be partial to* (*lift up the face of*) one nor *honor* (*hrd*) (*the face*) of the other. This rare verb to *honor* is found in 19:32 with *you shall defer to the old* (literally, *you shall honor the face of the old*).

In 19:16, if we act as *slanderers* (*rkil*) we can perpetrate injustices as severe as the misjudgments of 19:15.

The second half of 19:16 says *you shall not stand* (*against* or *beside*) *the blood of your neighbor*. The NRSV translates this as *you shall not profit by the blood of your neighbor*, using a complex parallel with Gen 27:40. Milgrom takes the *standing beside* as *standing aloof*. He notes that standing aloof can do as much harm or injustice at times as the slander mentioned in the same verse and the misjudgments mentioned in Lev 19:15.

19:17–18

These two verses are the climax of the ethical guidelines in 19:9–16 and the heart of the entire chapter. We are called on not to hate *anyone of our kin*; the Hebrew simply has the word *brother*, which can certainly mean *any Israelite of any clan* in context. Another general term for *people* or *neighbors* (*ym*) is used in 19:16 (do not be a slanderer *among your people*), 19:17 (you shall reprove *your neighbor*), and 19:18 (do not bear a grudge against *any of your people*). A third general term for *neighbor* (*reay*) is used in 19:16 (*profiting by the blood* of or *standing aloof* from *your neighbor*) and 19:18 (you shall love *your neighbor*). All these words should be taken in a broad sense; we can't put limits on whom we try not to hate or whom we try to love.

While we might think of hating and loving as unformed emotions, these two verses make more sense if we think of subsequent actions. Milgrom (1646) notes that "this hate is not just an emotion, but implies a mental activity, namely, plotting countermeasures." The phrase to not hate *in your heart* could also touch on this mental activity, since in the Hebrew comprehension of the body the heart was the seat of thinking as well as feeling. So Absalom silently hated his brother Amnon (2 Sam 13:22) and, after two full years, had Amnon killed. Zech 8:17 says, "Do not devise evil in your hearts against one another, and love no false oath."

In addition to not hating, we are called on to *reprove* (*ich*) one another, to take the initiative and honestly express and discuss serious differences in values with one another. The call to reprove is found in Prov 9:8; 10:17; 27:5–6. The three sayings indicate that someone who accepts a reproof will be better off in the long run. Note Prov 9:8, "the wise, when rebuked, will love you."

The Hebrew of Lev 19:17 has an intensive verb form, which could be translated *Reproving, you shall reprove* or *Surely, you shall reprove*. Sometimes translations, such as the NRSV, do not note the intensive form. Milgrom paraphrases *Reprove your fellow openly*, using *openly* to catch the intensive nuance.

Milgrom notes that reproving someone must be done out of love, as in *you shall love your neighbor* (19:18). Other motives such as pique, jealousy, or a desire to manipulate are totally unacceptable.

The Qumran community took this call to reprove as one of their main ways to build their community. But they went well beyond Lev 19 in requiring that community leaders be informed of reproofs by the reprovers, after which the leaders had to keep written records of these reports to monitor progress.

Lev 19:17 notes that if you do not reprove you will incur guilt yourself. The Hebrew has *do not lift up sin because of him* (the reproved one). Num 18:32 has the same Hebrew phrase with reference to a point of tithing: *you shall incur no guilt by reason of it* (*you shall not lift up sin because of it*). The importance of reproving, regardless of the outcome, is dramatically portrayed in Ezek 3:16–21.

The thinking in Lev 19:17 and in Ezek 3 is communal. If you have a God-given duty to reprove and you fail to do so, your community may well do something wrong because you have remained silent. The situation is easier to imagine with regard to parents and their children. If youngsters are not respectfully but appropriately reprimanded at key points, their later relationships as adults will be affected. Another way you might incur guilt by not reproving would be if you react in violence later on to wrongs done by the very people whom you did not reprove earlier.

Lev 19:18 touches on this subject of reacting in violence. Loving and reproving are the ideals. But we can also be tempted to *take vengeance* (*nqm*) or *bear a grudge* (*ntr*). Both Hebrew verbs are forceful; see Nah 1:2: "A jealous and avenging (*nqm*) God is the LORD, the LORD is avenging (*nqm*) and wrathful; the LORD takes vengeance (*nqm*) on his adversaries and rages (*ntr*) against his enemies." Note the final phrase. To *rage against one's enemies* is a more fitting phrase in this context than simply to translate that God *bears a grudge against* his enemies. Milgrom suggests that bearing a grudge can at times mean *seething in anger*. Most of us have had this experience.

We all know the closing phrase, *you shall love your neighbor as yourself*. Milgrom (1655) uses a paraphrase to explain the goal: "Love the good for your neighbor as you love the good for yourself." The paraphrase might be helpful, since it reminds us that all the good comes ultimately from God.

19:19

The reminders in 19:19 about not crossbreeding cattle, not mixing varieties of seed in one farm field, and not weaving fabric from two materials (normally linen and wool) might appear trivial or puzzling at first. There is not much point in looking for significant examples in nature. Crossing a horse and a donkey produces a mule; while that may be discouraged in Lev 19, centuries later mules became common work animals. Further, commentators assume the original reference was to cattle, not horses. Some plants or crops might interfere with each other if mixed together. One example is that peach and almond trees harm each other chemically when in proximity.

One reason why many ancient peoples combined linen with wool designs in fabrics was that wool was more easily dyed.

The passage in Deut 22:9–12, which mentions the same topics, seems to be modeled on Lev 19. One addition is that *tassels* (*gdlim*) should be added at the four corners of outer cloaks, but no explanation is offered there as to why. Milgrom assumes that D is calling for the tassels to be made of the same unmixed fibers that were used for the garment.

Instead of wondering about examples from nature, we should consider religious reasons for all this. It seems that Priestly authors and editors considered mixtures in nature to be more under God's control. Mixtures characterize the holiness of the sacred sphere and those authorized to enter and serve there, thus there are woven images of mixed fibers in some of the tabernacle and temple curtains, and sculpted figures in the temple. These images were mainly of *cherubim*. While we think of them as angels, the same word can refer to mythological beasts such as winged lions or bulls. These were icons that represented divine power in the abstract rather than specific deities. The high priest had several garments woven from blends of blue wool and white linen, and the ordinary priests had sashes made of the same material and colors.

Milgrom reminds us that in Num 15:37–40, a passage attributed to H, *fringes* (*zizit*) must be placed at the corners of garments, and are to have a blue woolen thread woven into them. Then God explains in Num 15:39–40, "You have the fringe so that, when you see it, you will remember all the commandments of the LORD, and do them, and not follow the lust of your own heart and your own eyes. So you shall remember and do my commandments, and you shall be holy to your God."

This one thread of wool could violate the law in Lev 19, as well as the later call for plain tassels in Deut 22, but Milgrom reminds us that using the blue wool might be a way of indicating that the laity shared in the calling of the high priest and the other priests and Levites. The people shared in the same calling to seek holiness throughout their lives. So the Holiness editor of Num 15 was making an important theological point; the little bits of blue wool linked all Israelites together.

19:20–22

The passage in 19:20–22 outlines a rare legal case, and seems at odds with the style of the rest of the chapter. We need to look briefly at the case itself and then find the reason why it is included in this chapter. Milgrom assumes that it was part of a Priestly document on marriage cases to start with, and was deliberately inserted here by H editors for their own purposes.

The owner of the woman slave and the person to whom she had been betrothed (or designated) are not identified; they are not the direct focus of this case, nor is the woman slave herself. The word *designated* (*hrp*) is rarely used with regard to marriage; perhaps it hints at lesser penalties. To be more precise, 19:20 notes that the woman had not been *ransomed* (*pdt*) by the future husband. The word can also be translated *redeemed* in many cases, but that translation has positive overtones best left out of this passage. The context here is strictly financial. The price for the woman had either not yet been clearly set or not yet collected. The mention of the possibility of her attaining her freedom from slavery in some other way is not developed, even though some slaves did attain their freedom without having the money to do so.

The main focus is on the outsider, the man who had sinful sexual relations with her. The woman may have been a willing or semi-willing participant; rape does not have to be proved. Still, the greater blame rests on the outsider; as a freeman, he had more power than the woman.

The context could lead to the conclusion that all the parties are Israelites. In 25:39–43 H calls on Israel to avoid making any Israelite a slave for any reason, but this earlier Priestly passage was simply borrowed in its entirety.

The owner had already made arrangements for the woman to be given in marriage, most likely to become a slave wife to another. In one sense the original owner is only a partial owner now, and the law does not concern itself with any compensation for him. The woman and the outsider do not qualify for the death penalties of adultery, since she was still a slave and not yet with her betrothed. All this—the status of the woman, and the identity and responsibility of the outsider—must be clarified and confirmed by an *inquiry* (*bqrt*).

In the ancient Near East adultery was often considered both a civil and a religious offense. Note the remark of Abimelech to Abraham, "What have you done to us? How have I sinned against you, that you have brought such *great sin* on me and my kingdom?" (the NRSV has *great guilt*.) Lev 18:20 and 18:25–30, as a summary of all of Lev 18, certainly think of the national desecration and sinful dimensions brought on by adultery and improper relationships.

In Israel the Sinai covenant bound everyone regarding many major sins, including adultery. Milgrom remarks that the outsider is certainly guilty in God's eyes, even if not liable for death on the case level. The offender must bring a *guilt offering* (*asam*) for his expiation.

There were two usual ways to atone for great sins: death (not applicable under the highly unusual technicalities of this case), or sacrifices for inadvertent sins (which this was not). Still, some mechanism for atonement, some sort of sacrifice, was needed.

The *guilt offering* of a ram is mentioned three times in 19:21–22. Milgrom uses *penalty* the first time and *reparation offering* the other two times. Guilt offerings for sins that are confessed, and thereby reclassified as inadvertent sins, are mentioned in 5:6, 15; 6:6. At times fees may replace the animal sacrifice (5:15, 18; 6:6), but not in this case in Lev 19.

As in earlier parts of this chapter, the H editors are pointing out that major desecrations of God's holiness must be addressed first. No other pious practices will avail until the underlying or major sin is expiated.

19:23–25

The next several sections may be treated more quickly. In the Near East even today orchard trees and grapevines need several years to mature before they can produce reliable yields. In biblical Hebrew grapevines were also referred to as trees. Milgrom mentions four- or five-year stages for almond and date trees, five to seven years for figs and pomegranates, and three to six for grapevines.

During the immature stage, blossoms and buds should be removed early each season, since growing buds and stunted fruit is a significant waste of energy for the entire plant. The branches are not pruned; the buds and blossoms are simply plucked by hand. The Hebrew uses an oddly religious vocabulary here, likening the treatment of the trees to *circumcision*, and what is *forbidden* is called *uncircumcised*.

Milgrom argues that another custom lies behind these guidelines. He brings up biblical and rabbinic references to annual festive ceremonies involving first grapes and new wine, and speculates that the H editors wanted to downplay those overenthusiastic festivals by shifting or broadening the topic to include fruit and nut trees.

The most unusual regulation (perhaps also part of the downplaying) is in 19:24, where the entire fourth-year crop should be set aside for the LORD. That would mean that the entire crop would be used by the priests and their families. It is possible that this setting aside is the act of holiness that H is proposing, dedicating a year's crop to God and delaying the benefit or income from the trees for one year. Milgrom doubts that the majority of Israelites ever brought these crops to the sanctuary as described here.

19:26–28

The next three verses refer to many improper attempts to contact demons or ancestral spirits. Milgrom takes the command not to eat *any meat with its blood* to be better translated *any meat over its blood*, as we saw earlier. What is being condemned is the pouring of the blood into the ground as a way of summoning demons or the spirits of the dead.

The H editors consistently ban attempts at *augury* (*nhs*) or *divination* (*ywn*). The latter is translated *witchcraft* in the NRSV of 19:26 (see 17:7; 18:21; 19:31; 20:1–6, 27). In these rituals one seeks to learn the future.

From a comfortable distance, we might argue that augury or divination could be compatible with monotheism, and even with a belief in prophecy. At one point even the high priest used two special stones (the *urim* and *thummim*) to cast lots to seek some idea of God's will.

But this is armchair speculation. In fact divination easily leads to *sorcery*, wherein one seeks to change the future by coercing blessings or curses from the gods. Even if one were to intend a plan of blessing (what we call white magic) to one of cursing (black magic), the whole point of sorcery is incompatible with monotheism at any level. See Ezek 13 for an extended diatribe against anyone who tries to interfere with God's plans and messages.

Shaving and cutting hair in a destructive way, even if for mourning, was seen as a gesture against the forces of life. Normal trimming was allowed.

Gashing one's skin was a part of intensive prayer rituals in Baal worship. In many other cultures it was associated with mourning, perhaps thought of as a way of disguising the living so evil spirits could not harm them.

Tattooing was at times a symbol of dedication to a specific god or cult. In many societies it was a way of marking slaves (see Exod 21:6; Deut 15:17). As we noted earlier, H wished Israelites to be spared the shame of slavery (Lev 25:39–43), although resident aliens and foreigners were left out (Lev 25:44–46).

All these superstitions, attempts to know the future, and excessive mourning rites drain us of the energy to be holy, the energy to try to appreciate how holy God is and to try to imitate his goodness.

19:29

Obviously, forcing a daughter into prostitution is demeaning and sinful. Milgrom affirms that the majority of scholars doubt that there was much cultic prostitution in the ancient Near East—that is, the sponsoring of sexual encounters with designated shrine personnel of the opposite gender as an integral part of a belief system. The Semitic root word traditionally taken to mean *female cult prostitute* (*qdsh*) may have also been used for women who were instead *wet nurses* or *midwives*.

Milgrom suggests that there were prostitutes living close to local shrines; we might call them "shrine followers." The command "do not *profane* (*hll*) your daughter" is matched in 21:9 by another surprising statement, "When the daughter of a priest *profanes herself* through prostitution, she *profanes* her father; she shall be burned to death." In 21:7 a priest is not allowed to marry a *harlot* (*zonah*) or a woman who has been *profaned*.

The rationale at the end of 19:28 is that "the land not become *prostituted* (*znh*) and full of *depravity* (*zmh*)." The last word can be taken in a sexual sense in itself; Milgrom suggests we use the word *lewdness*.

While we are sure there was no cultic prostitution within Judaism, Milgrom's profile of shrine followers and of some of the warnings regarding the daughters and wives of shrine priests reminds us of some less than holy situations. Milgrom admits that everyone probably knew who the shrine followers were, and why they were there. The women may have made periodic donations to the shrine to keep everyone looking the other way. At times a priest at a local shrine may have become romantically involved with one of these women. After all, they were not demons; throughout history many women have made the transition from prostitution to marriage, and should not be judged by society solely for the earlier stage in their lives.

The Holiness editors were deeply concerned about all this. They were trying to prevent more fathers from forcing their daughters. They were worried that the depravity would spread and offend God all the more.

19:30–32

The next three verses could be taken as the original conclusion to the chapter. Specifically, 19:3 and 30 both mention the *Sabbath*. *Parents* are mentioned in 19:3 and the *elderly* in 19:32. The phrase *do not turn* is used only twice in this chapter: for *idols* in 19:4 and for *mediums* and *wizards* in 19:31.

The mention of the *sanctuary* in 19:30 can be taken as the complement to the *Sabbath*. The Sabbath, commanded in the Decalog, is the foundation for sacred times, and the sanctuary provides the sacred space. Ezek 23:38 speaks of the double desecration of Sabbath and sanctuary: sacrificing children to Molech at the ravine below the temple, and then entering the temple itself on the same day for regular Sabbath worship.

The *mediums* (*awbth*) and the *wizards* (*idyni*) practice divination, mainly necromancy (communicating with someone's ancestral spirits). The priests consistently condemned the practice, but it remained a popular custom. Even today some people search for fortune tellers or spiritualists rather than more proven counselors.

The call to respect the elderly in 19:32 is self-evident. The reference to *fearing your God* might be a hint that God will punish any disrespect shown the elderly.

19:33-34

We find many references in the Pentateuch and elsewhere to the *gerim*, *resident aliens*. They were second-class citizens, to use a modern term. Milgrom notes that it took many decades, or even centuries, for some groups of aliens to become fully incorporated within Israel, and that often happened mainly by intermarriage.

Ideally, each Israelite was to love aliens, not oppress them—to support them, include them in festivals, allow them rest on the Sabbath, and provide them safety. The aliens in turn were to follow the same rules if they participated in sacrifices, and they had to follow the same major religious prohibitions about leaven, animal blood, etc.

The command *not to oppress* (*inh*) can mean *not to cheat* in 25:14, 17. It could well mean that here also, given the following verses on false weights and measures. The very command to love the alien must include specific actions, just as did the command to love your neighbor in 19:18.

19:35-36a

It was a universal temptation to misrepresent weights, volumes, or lengths in business dealings. But the fact that "everybody" did it did not make it right, then or now. Milgrom notes that in ancient Greece officials policed the marketplaces, making random checks of merchants' scales and weights.

The note about trustworthy weights and measures in Lev 19:35-36 appears again in a later, copied form in Deut 25:13-16. In our passage, note the drum-roll effect of using the adjective *honest* (or *just*, from the noun *zedek*) four times in 19:36. The Hebrew uses *of justice* in an adjectival sense; it reads, "Balances of justice, weights of justice, an ephah of justice, and a hin of justice shall be to you."

19:36b-37

This closing pronouncement could focus just on 19:35-36a, or it might reflect back to 18:2b-5, which also mentions the Egyptians. Both passages speak of *statutes* and *ordinances* in solemn tones, so 19:36b-37 helps link all of Lev 18-19 together. Given the opening of the next chapter, *Say further to the people of Israel*, and some of the concluding verses in 20:22–26 (especially 20:22, which speaks of statutes and ordinances), and considering the great amount of repetition in the content of Lev 20 in line with Lev 18–19, we could say that all three chapters are strongly interlinked.

Conclusion

Milgrom provides his readers with a review of the theology of holiness, which focuses on Lev 19. What follows is my attempt to reword and represent the gist of his review.

Milgrom speaks of the traces of animism in other ancient Near Eastern cultures. In animism there are always links between humanity and divinity, and some of the links are independent demonic forces. These demons can be a danger to humans, and even to certain gods. There is no significant animism in Judaism, no independent demon. Holiness belongs to God alone; holiness is his nature. He makes anything else holy, and he can always relent and declare something impure or unholy.

So when Old Testament editors use nouns or verbs for *holiness* they mean *set apart for God*. Priestly editors think of certain spaces, persons, or times as set apart, and of the central role of religious ritual for the nation.

Holiness editors made three refinements in their understanding of holiness. First, gradations between laity and priests are lowered. Priests and laity (folk priesthood) all must strive for holiness. Second, holiness involves obeying prohibitions but it also involves performing ethical acts. Third, everyone needs to be aware of how large the sphere of religious and ethical goals can be. Lev 19 serves as a panoramic overview of this sphere. Further, we are called on to make the sphere ever larger, to turn more encounters with the common into encounters with holiness. Milgrom (1717) remarks, "thus for H, holiness is a dynamic concept, toward which all of Israel, priests and laity alike, must continuously strive: priests to retain it, lay persons to attain it."

Milgrom considers Deuteronomic (D) theology fairly parallel with that of H, but he notes that D goes further in grounding the holiness of all the people in the original Sinai covenant. But at many points in Deuteronomy it is clear that *if* Israel obeys the commandments, *only then* will God fulfill his promise of holiness to the forefathers (see Deut 26:16–19;

28:9). Deut 26:16–19 is essential for our understanding of the mutuality of the Sinai covenant.

Milgrom explains the relationship between H and D this way: in D holiness is the reason for laws, while in H the laws are the means to holiness. The high point of this optimism in H is Lev 19. Milgrom (1723) notes, "In Lev 19, H, in effect, writes a new 'Decalogue.' YHWH's self-declaration becomes a call to holiness, followed by a series of commandments (addressing the most pressing problems in H's time . . .) by which holiness may be achieved."

Prophets also spoke about God's holiness and the laws we need to embrace, though at times they seem more discouraged by Israel's failings. For Milgrom, Lev 19 is a deeply hopeful profile of how we are called and supported by God as we strive to live up to our calling.

Section Sixteen

LEVITICUS 20:1–27

Questions

77. If you were writing a history of Ancient Israel, what would you assume from reading 20:1–5?

78. Do you see any logical or theological contradictions between 20:7 and 20:8? Explain.

79. What are your first impressions about the content and, even more, the style of 20:9–21?

80. Note the remark ending 20:24b: I am the LORD your God; I have separated you from the peoples. This could wrap up 20:22–24a, but it also introduces 20:25–26. Why does God fall back to a few general dietary regulations during this major climax (20:24b–26) to the entire chapter?

We shift gears somewhat in Lev 20, reviewing and expanding the subjects of Lev 18. Some scholars assume that Lev 20 was a direct continuation of Lev 18. Certainly much of the vocabulary and style is the same. They note that 18:2–5 and 18:24–30 flank the main topics in 18:6–23; in like manner we can take 20:7–8 and 20:22–26 to flank the main topics in 20:9–21.

Another school of thought is that Lev 20 was an independent or separate tradition, selected by the H editors. To support this proposal, commentators note fine points about differences in the penalties and participants between the two chapters. For instance, the topics of cursing parents (20:9) and using mediums or wizards (20:6, 27) do not appear in Lev 18. A more important difference is the matter of the penalties themselves. In Lev 18 the only penalties mentioned are that Israel could be vomited out of the land (18:28) or that individuals will be *cut off* (18:29). The last phrase refers to God's intention for someone's name and descendants to fail more than to that person being totally shunned by everyone. In Lev 20 there is a range of legal executions by the community (20:9–16), a few mentions of being cut off (20:17–18), or of remaining childless (20:20–21). Further, the lone earlier reference to Molech sacrifices (18:21) is significantly expanded (20:2–5).

Milgrom asks why Lev 18 and 20 were not simply joined together by editors. The answer is that if we take Lev 19 as a key chapter in Leviticus and in the entire Pentateuch, then Lev 18 and 20 could have been used to set off and highlight Lev 19. The editors may have chosen these independent warnings about Molech sacrifices and sexual wrongs because they were so destructive of holiness, and placed them to add all the more impact to the "new Decalogue," Milgrom's term for Lev 19 as a whole. My term for Lev 19, in answer to question 76, is "Utopia of Holiness."

We can outline Lev 20 as follows:

20:1	Introduction
20:2–5	Penalties for Molech sacrifices
20:6	Penalties for using mediums or wizards
20:7–8	Motivation clauses for 20:9–21
20:9	Penalty for cursing parents
20:10–21	Penalties for forbidden sexual relationships
20:22–26	Further motivation clauses in concluding Lev 20
20:27	Death sentence for a medium or wizard

20:2–5

The phrase *any of their offspring* in 20:2 could refer to any infants under the control of the paterfamilias, including grandchildren or even great-grandchildren. The one doing the sacrificing is committing idolatry and murder; the stoning is certainly for the latter (Num 35:31–34). Psalm 106:34–39 recounts the same tragedy. In addition God will *cut off* those who make these sacrifices, since they *profane his holy name* by wrongly assuming that God does not object to such worship of Molech.

God goes even further by promising to punish those who sacrifice offspring, should *the people of the land* fail to put them to death. He will punish *them and all who follow them in prostituting themselves to Molech*. The phrase *people of the land* in 20:4 should include the resident aliens. The Hebrew has *closing, they close their eyes*; this intensive form stresses the deliberate way people have of ignoring "the elephant in the room," to use a modern idiom. God will punish the *families* of Molech worshippers, that is, the *extended kin groups*.

This death sentence can only be carried out if there were witnesses to the sacrifice of the infant. Milgrom characterizes *the people of the land* in Lev 20 as "any unofficial, unauthorized body of Israelites.... In reality, we are dealing—to use a derogatory term—with a lynch mob.... The sinner must be killed *immediately*; any delay jeopardizes the welfare of the entire nation" (1731–32).

20:6

The words for *mediums* (*awbt*) and *wizards* (*idyni*) in 20:6 can also mean the *spirits of the dead* themselves. At times context does not give much help to translators. Milgrom argues that in 20:6 (and in 19:31) we should think of *the spirits of the dead*. He notes that the Hebrew of 20:27 can also be translated as "a man or a woman *when there is in them the spirits of the dead* shall surely die." The mediums and wizards, like those appeasing Molech, are trying to consult the dead to find out what the future will bring.

20:7–8

Milgrom takes 20:7–8 as an introduction to what follows in 20:9–21. One could also think of it as a bridge paragraph, pointing back to the unholy practices of idolatry, especially with Molech, and forward to the unholy relationships of 20:9–21.

Here in 20:7 the Israelites are called on to *make themselves holy* or *consecrate themselves*. This is a reflexive form of the verb *qdsh*. In this form it must mean something like *behave as people who have been consecrated*, or *put yourselves into a pure state, religiously and ethically*. In

20:8 God says *I am the one sanctifying you*, which is a causative form of the same verb. In this form God must be the subject, not the people themselves.

We can understand how the two somewhat contradictory statements can be next to each other if we remember that the main way the Israelites can make themselves holy is by obeying God's commandments. And God can say *I am the one sanctifying you* because he had given them the commandments in the first place (see Exod 31:13; Ezek 20:12).

Milgrom goes on to ask where this conviction of the Holiness editors came from, this "democratization" that everyone is called on to strive for holiness. He points to the economic troubles at the end of the eighth century BCE, as hinted at in 25:25–43. As small farmers lost their independence and were reduced to near serfdom, Holiness editors may have tried to raise their hopes that they were still valued in the eyes of God. Milgrom calls this a "spiritual, metaphysical holiness . . . neither financial success nor social prestige nor priestly pedigree was a prerequisite for its attainment. Only adherence to the divine commandments was required. By observing them, an Israelite would become holy" (1741).

20:9

All the family relationships go back to one's father and mother; without respect for them all else could go downhill. Even Philo noted that this disrespect for parents could certainly include verbal abuse. Stern punishments are also called for in Deut 21:18–21; Exod 21:17, but there had to be credible witnesses. Chances are that few if any sons were ever actually executed in accord with these laws.

20:10

The *neighbor* is most likely another Israelite. The community must make the decision, not the offended husband. There must be witnesses; otherwise punishment is left to God. Commentators speculate that originally the punishment may have been just for the man.

20:13

Milgrom notes that "Israel's territory was pocketed by numerous Canaanite enclaves, not to speak of more populous nations on its borders. It was understandable that Israel was obsessed with increasing its birth rate without endangering harmonious relations within the extended family, especially among those who lived in the same household" (1750).

20:14

It is possible that the woman and her mother agreed at the same point to live with the man.

20:17

The subject is a biological half sister, not a stepsister not born to one's mother or father. It seems that the relationship was mutual and perhaps even undertaken in secrecy; thus there would be no witnesses who could call for the death penalty.

20:18

The *sickness* (*dwh*) refers to *menstruation*, even though this is an incorrect correlation. See Lam 1:13; 5:17, where the same word respectively means *physically faint* or *sick of heart*. Milgrom suggests that perhaps the woman's physical infirmity represents her figurative infirmity, as a vulnerable widow or divorcee, a potential prey to the males in her household.

20:19

These are full sisters of the mother or father, not in-laws.

20:20

This is the father's brother's wife. There was no similar prohibition about a mother's brother's wife.

20:22–26

As we have noted, H could have added this exhortation to Lev 20 with Lev 18 in mind. Parallels include the following:

- Lev 20:22a repeats some of 20:8 and also 18:4–5. We could take the two units (20:22 and 18:4–5) as bookends around the enclosed passages, esp. Lev 19.
- Lev 20:22b repeats some of 18:28.
- Lev 20:23 echoes parts of 18:3, 24, 27.

The second half of 20:24, *I am the LORD your God; I have separated you from the peoples*, begins a new theme which runs into the next two verses.

The same verb to *separate* (*bdl*) is used four times in this paragraph:

20:24	*I have separated* you from the peoples
20:25	*you shall make a distinction* between the clean and unclean
20:25	*I have set apart* for you to hold unclean
20:26	*I have separated* you from the peoples

The emphasis on Israel being a separate nation, with very restrictive dietary laws, is part of God's larger plan. There is much more to holiness than dietary laws; Lev 19 demonstrates that. God's plan to use Israel as a separate nation only makes sense if they become holy, so that they can be an example to the rest of the world. Milgrom (1761) notes that "the separation of Israel from the nations is a sine qua non for the maintenance of order *within the human world*." In Gen 1:4, 7, 14 the Priestly writers say that God *separated* (*bdl*) light from darkness, and the waters below from the waters above. The sun, moon, and stars separate the day from the night. As Milgrom remarks, "separation creates order, and the distinctions between the elements must be maintained lest the world collapse into chaos and confusion."

20:27

In 20:6 those ordinary people who attempt to consult spirits of the dead will be cut off. In 20:27 the professional male or female medium or wizard must be executed. Milgrom suggests that 20:6 describes a "user," and 20:27 describes a "pusher," to borrow modern terms.

Conclusion

Commentators note the centuries long resistance to the Priestly calls for an end to divination and other forms of necromancy and ancestor worship, even if the human sacrifices to Molech were eliminated more quickly. Milgrom (1772) states, "the battle against necromancy formed a distinct phase in the monotheistic revolution, a battle—to judge by the Biblical record—that was never won."

There were different purposes in trying to contact the ancestors. The ancestral spirits were sought to grant favors, or to placate them if they were angry. Reciting their names was a way to keep the spirits alive in some sense.

Various minor ceremonies were connected with ancestor worship in general: placing or eating certain foods near the graves, reciting the names of the beloved dead, offering small sacrifices of animals or plants, or the worshipping of small figurines, especially of the royal line. Deut 26:14 and Isa 57:6 hint at food offerings or sacrifices.

It seems that biblical authors were willing to consider these food offerings as a form of veneration, not adoration. Milgrom (1776) asks, "What choice had they, considering that any attempt to ban them would have been totally ignored by the populace? The hitherto long, uninterrupted tradition in the ancient Near East, that worshipping the dead would guarantee their guardianship of and benefactions to their living descendants, continued unabated."

Christian missionaries have run into the same problems over the centuries, and have used the same technique of tamping down ancestor worship and turning it into lesser forms of veneration.

But the professional necromancers went too far. They infringed on God's sovereignty and on his use of prophets. Isa 8:19–20; 57:5–10 show some of the prophetic disapproval of various forms of necromancy, while

Deut 18:10-22 is the classic passage denouncing divination and false prophecy.

Section Seventeen

LEVITICUS 21:1—22:33

Questions

81. Is the wife included in the funeral restrictions for a priest in 21:1–3?
82. What do you make of the phrase *food of God* in 21:6, 8, 17, 21, 22; 22:25? The same word for *food* (*lhm*) is also used in 22:7, 11, 13, where it refers to food for the priests and their families.
83. Who gains by the observing of all these rules in 21:1–15?
84. In 22:17–25 why must every sacrificial animal be held to the same norm? What's so wrong with sacrificing a blind animal, to take one example?
85. Consider 22:26–30 as it is written—a direct speech from God. It would help to read the verses aloud. What picture do you get of God, as you reflect on this jumble of five verses?
86. What is odd about the 22:32 phrase *that I may be sanctified among the people of Israel?*

The next two chapters of Leviticus can be studied as one unit, since they deal mainly with the priesthood and religious ceremonies. The section in each chapter on blemishes is one structural link between the two chapters. We could outline the two chapters this way:

21:1   Introduction

21:2–9   Purity regulations for priests

21:10–15	Purity regulations for high priest
21:16–23	Blemish restrictions for priests
21:24	Conclusion
22:1–9	Regulations for priests about sacred donations (of food)
22:10–16	Regulations for laity about the same sacred donations
22:17–25	Blemish restrictions for sacrificial animals
22:26–30	Additional details about sacrifices
22:31–33	Conclusion

Many of these instructions are for the priests; their call to serve does involve more obligations. The refrain about *the LORD sanctifying* at the end of 20:8; 21:8, 15, 23; 22:9, 16, 32 is another binding technique, tying much of the content together. Lev 20:8 and 22:32 refer to all Israel. Another four citations refer to the priests, although these references are not all clear at first. Finally, 21:23 seems to refer to holy objects, mainly the curtain and the altar.

Milgrom notes that in Israel the hereditary priests did not take on just a few simple tasks, as did their appointed counterparts in most other ancient Near Eastern cultures. The priests of Israel had to know, teach, and perform a very complex legacy of law and ritual, most of which was comprehended by the people at large. Their own priestly lives were closely observed by those among whom they lived and served, and their own ritual purity was a vital necessity for all the rituals. Milgrom (1796) refers to their "extensive schooling, on the one hand, and disciplined practice, on the other."

21:1b–6

These restrictions on priests about being near a corpse or attending funerals for any but their immediate family may be surprising, but they do fit into the larger system of what is clean or unclean. Basically, the priests could not have significant roles at any funeral.

The references in 21:5 against cutting hair or scarring the body make a sharp contrast to well-known pagan practices. In many other cultures hair was considered one of the locations for life forces, and locks of hair were used to represent self-sacrifice and to invoke blessings on the dead. Scarring or gashing the flesh seems to have had the same ceremonial logic as the cutting of hair, a way of offering up some life force. All Israelites were to avoid these polytheistic practices.

Lev 21:6 echoes 20:26 in form. In 21:6 the warning is that profaning a sacrifice would forfeit a priest's holiness right away.

21:7–9

The concern for proper marriages disqualified various classes of women: ones who had been known to be promiscuous earlier on, Gentiles, divorcees, and even women who had been raped. Some of these women were excluded more for matters of reputation than for questionable virginity; after all, widows could marry ordinary priests. Unfortunately, women bore more of the social stigma than men for promiscuity, divorce, and rape. In 21:9 brazenly promiscuous daughters of priests were especially condemned; this verse may have also covered ordinary premarital sex as well as prostitution. This condemnation may have come about because if the daughters ate of sacred portions set aside for the families of priests they would profane the sacrifice.

In the closing phrase of 21:8, *I the LORD, I who sanctify you, am holy*, the plural pronoun *you* likely refers to the priests, despite the confusion of pronouns.

21:10–15

These pre-exilic regulations for the high priest are even more demanding. He may not marry a widow or anyone outside the clans or the tribe of Levi. Were he to do so, any children of that marriage would been dishonored, as mentioned in 21:15.

He may never attend any funeral, even for his own parents. The command for him *not to go outside the sanctuary* may refer to going to a funeral, or it might mean the larger area adjacent to the sanctuary, where the high priest normally lived with his own family.

21:16–23

Concern for blemishes among priests offering sacrifices is found in most ancient Near Eastern cultures. Milgrom suggests that this list in 21 is modeled on the animal list in Lev 22.

Some argue that 21:23 may refer only to the high priest; if so, the word translated *sanctuaries* should instead be taken as *sacred things* (specifically the curtain and the altar). They would be the things of which God says *I sanctify them*.

The restrictions on priests for physical blemishes are extensive. Some, such as blindness or unusual shortness of stature, might seem fair or at least practical, but the long list of those who may not perform ceremonial duties certainly includes many deformed and ill brought to that state by God himself. The thoroughness of the restrictions spurs us to imagine thousands of blemished, when there might have only been dozens. Recall the similar banishment of those Israelites with scale diseases and bleeding disorders, who had to stay outside the camp. Like them, the blemished priests were simultaneously called and banished. All we can say is that, for the Holiness editors, God set higher standards for his chosen people—physical standards representing an ethical worldview.

Milgrom puts it this way: "The priestly system of impurities / blemishes is . . . an arbitrary set of rules reflecting some higher set of values—in the case of impurity, that Israel should choose life (God's laws) over the forces of death (the violation of God's laws), and in the case of blemishes, that YHWH's sphere of holiness demands moral and ritual perfection" (1839).

The Qumran sect added several more disqualifications: one for those priests not able to read Torah passages aloud effectively, and others for priests who had lived abroad, either of their own will or as prisoners of war.

21:24

By mentioning *all the people of Israel* H again charges the laity to hold the priests and the high priest to account for how they perform their duties and how they seek holiness in their own priestly lives.

22:2–9

After blemishes we move on to clean and unclean states for priests. Some of these unclean states were of short duration. Lev 22:2 tells the priests to *deal carefully* with the sacred donations. The verb (*nzr*) means to *separate oneself* or to *make distinctions*; in short, to *treat something with awe*.

The pronouns *you* and *he* in 22:3 refer to priests. Priests may not eat of animals that have died naturally or by wild predators (22:8), while lay people who do the same need only undergo minor purifications (17:15).

The warning to priests in 22:9 echoes what follows in 22:15–16.

22:10–16

In 22:10 the *lay person* (*zr*) is an outsider, not a servant or immediate family member of a priest. The same verse also speaks of *a bound or hired servant* of a priest (*toshab cohen sakir*). The Hebrew is difficult, and has been traditionally taken to mean two categories of employee. Milgrom takes it as a hendiadys to represent one category—the *resident hireling* of a priest. The hireling can support himself and his family from his wages. Lev 22:11 refers to a non-Israelite slave in the classic sense, who has no independent means to support himself or his family. There is no clear indication that this slave was circumcised, as would be expected.

In 22:12–13 the widowed or divorced childless daughters of a priest may live at home as dependents and eat of the food provided for the priest and his dependents. Lev 22:14 refers to laity.

Finally, 22:15–16 refer to priests, who could mistake which animal is being sacrificed for which reason, and consequently err in distributing the portions. Any such mix-up must be avoided at all costs; it must not become a routine error.

22:17–25

Lev 22:18 indicates clearly that the laity along with the priests are responsible for unblemished sacrificial animals. A minor exception is made in 22:23 for animals in freewill offerings—the sacrifices offered in quick response for significant blessings.

In 22:24–25 gelded animals were forbidden for the altar. The phrase in 22:24 *within your land* might in context mean *within (any shrine sanctuary) in your land.* Nor could gelded animals be purchased from foreigners or offered on their behalf (22:25).

There seems to have been no prohibition on gelding in general; it was and still is a part of standard herd management and husbandry.

22:26–30

The custom of not slaughtering new animals for seven days (Lev 22:27) also occurs in Exod 22:30, but there seems to be no convincing way to explain the custom. The rule in Lev 22:28 might have been a humanitarian one. In 22:29–30 the time limit for consuming a thanksgiving sacrifice might be in a stylistic balance to the time limitations for well-being sacrifices in 19:5–8.

22:31–33

This paragraph applies to all of Lev 22, and echoes segments of 19:2, 36–37.

The phrase in 22:32 *that I may be sanctified among the people of Israel* needs some explanation. How can God be sanctified by anyone else? Milgrom suggests, "YHWH is sanctified when Israel performs his commandments. . . . Israel increasingly regards him with sanctity and is more scrupulous in preventing the desecration of his name. . . . The result is that YHWH's sanctity is more visible, giving the appearance of his increased sanctity" (1888).

For 22:32b–33 the NRSV has "I am the LORD; I sanctify you, I who *brought you out* of the land of Egypt to be your God: I am the LORD." Milgrom (1845, 1888–90) translates 22:32b–33 as "I am YHWH who sanctifies you, your *deliverer (hmwzia)* from the land of Egypt to be your God; I am YHWH."

Deliverer can be taken as a participle (from *iza*) in parallel with the last words of 22:32b, *who sanctifies you (meqqaddishkem)*. Both participles can be considered in context to be in the present tense. The same participle meaning *deliverer* can be found in Exod 6:7, where the NRSV has "who *has freed you (hmwzia)* from the burdens of the Egyptians."

Milgrom's point in taking these verb forms in the present tense is that God is continuously the sanctifier and deliverer of Israel; he provides, through his commandments, the means by which Israel can attain holiness.

The same theme can be seen in the refrain of God *sanctifying* Israel in 20:7–8 and 22:33, and the several repetitions of the refrain throughout Lev 21–22. God continues to bless and guide; his people need to know that this is his intention, and should act by using his gifts.

Section Eighteen

LEVITICUS 23:1–44

Questions

87. Taking 23:1–8 as a unit, what is the role of 23:3? What is the role of 23:4?

88. Comment on the style of 23:9–14. You could give the same response about the next passage, 23:15–21.

89. Comment on the style of 23:26–32 in comparison to your answer to the previous question.

90. Using just 23:33–36, what do you learn about the Festival of Booths?

91. Taking into account 23:39–43, what more do you learn about the Festival of Booths?

We can safely assume that Lev 23 is a later redaction of Priestly traditions by Holiness editors. It is a direct adaptation of Num 28–29. Various forms of the phrase *offering by fire* (*isseh*) can be found in Lev 23:8, 13, 18, 25, 27, 36 (twice), 37 (Milgrom prefers *food offering*). The phrase is used when H agrees with Num 28–29, but details are added in Lev 23 when H calls for different quantities or types of sacrifices in some cases.

Lev 23 lists the main events of the yearly liturgical calendar, but is addressed to the people at large. Second plural verb forms predominate, such as *you shall present offerings by fire* (in other verses the object is *burnt offerings* or *offerings of well-being*). The priests are mentioned just a few times (23:11, 20). The thrust of this chapter is that the people oversee the ceremonies; they are not to let themselves be passive observers of mysterious rites.

We can see a progression in Lev 21–23. The previous two chapters deal with ritual regulations for the priests and the people and their offerings; this chapter focuses on the times for each festival. The times had to be exact, and working during prohibited times was another form of desecration or blemish.

Num 10:10 mentions that some of the festivals were heralded by blowing notes or fanfares on the *shofar*, the instrument made from a ram's horn.

Lev 23 can be outlined as follows:

23:1–2	Introduction
23:3	Emphasis on Sabbaths
23:4	Continuation of the introduction
23:5–8	Passover and Unleavened Bread regulations
23:9–14	Offering of first barley sheaves
23:15–22	Offering of first wheat sheaves
23:23–25	New moon of seventh month
23:26–32	Day of Atonement
23:33–36	Festival of Ingathering or Booths
23:37–38	Summary
23:39–43	Additional remarks about Festival of Booths
23:44	Conclusion

The mention of the importance of Sabbaths is a carefully edited section. Note the layout of 23:2b–4, as Milgrom displays it:

[2b] These are the appointed festivals of the LORD that you shall proclaim
    as holy convocations
        my appointed festivals.
           [3] Six days
                work shall be done;

> but the seventh day is a Sabbath of complete rest, a
> holy convocation;
> you shall do no work;
> it is a Sabbath to the LORD throughout your settlements.
> ⁴ These are the appointed festivals of the LORD,
> the holy convocations,
> which you shall celebrate at the time appointed for them.

In this section the term *holy convocation* (*mqra qdsh*) is used three times and the term *appointed festival* (*moed*) is used four times. In the last case the NRSV paraphrases it as *at the time appointed for them*. Thus each and every Sabbath is an appointed festival, a holy convocation, and a day of complete rest (*shabbat shabbaton*). The Hebrew intensive idiom means *a Sabbath of Sabbath rest*. It is to be observed *throughout your settlements* (a phrase also used in 23:14, 21, 31). Finally, in 23:3 there is no mention of *offerings by fire*, which are mentioned for several of the other feasts.

While the beginning reader might assume that this emphasis on Sabbaths is traditional, in Priestly language Sabbaths are so entrenched in God's creation of the world that they don't need to be *appointed* or *convoked*. (One can translate "Sabbath *of* the LORD" rather than "Sabbath *to* the LORD" in 23:3.) There is never any doubt about how many days there are until the next Sabbath. Further, each Sabbath at the temple did involve morning and evening animal sacrifices, not mentioned in 23:3.

Milgrom argues that 23:3 is an interpolation, artfully encased between the verse before and after. He notes that in 23:37–38 Sabbaths are grouped with ceremonies involving individuals—gifts, votive offerings, free-will offerings—and all these are events that do not need to be appointed or convoked or to be assigned a proper day (the Hebrew of 23:37 has *the event of a day on its own day*).

23:4

The word *moed* for *appointed festival* does occur in discussions of the Sabbath in Num 28:2 and 29:39, but these are also passages from H.

The verb for *celebrate* in Lev 23:4 (*qra*) is the same as the word for *proclaim* in 23:2. The noun for *convocation* (*mqra*) is derived from this verb. The phrase *holy convocation* appears in 23:2, 3, 4, 7, 8, 21, 24, 27, 35, 36, 37.

Seven specific days are called holy convocations:

- The first and seventh day of Unleavened Bread (23:7–8)
- The day of the offering of the wheat sheaves (23:21)
- The first day of the seventh month (23:24)
- The day of Atonement (23:27)
- The first and eighth day of Booths (23:35, 36).

If the seven specific days are based on the importance of the number seven, that might be another argument for the later interpolation of 23:3. One can't have every Sabbath be such a special convocation all year long.

Priests had to keep fine-tuning the national calendar each year since lunar months are 29.5 days long and some months have to have 30 days to keep the months in balance. Every third year an additional month had to be added to keep the lunar calendar in line with the solar seasons. Modern synagogal calendars still use these calculations.

23:5–8

Pesach (or Passover) and the week for Unleavened Bread were ancient ceremonies that may have originally had to do with blessings on herds and crops. The foundation passages are Exod 12–20 for Passover and Num 28:17–25 for Unleavened Bread. The unleavened bread was made with old grain.

The noun *pesach* means *protection* rather than the traditional alternative *passing over*. It is not a holy convocation because work was allowed, and originally the meal was held at home.

Milgrom suggests that in early traditions the men, as heads of households, might have made a one-day round trip to local shrines the morning after the Pesach meal to begin the Unleavened Bread ceremonies. As that celebration was eventually extended to one week, perhaps as a balance to the festival of Ingathering, the closing day of convocation was simply held in the settlements so that no one had to make a second trip to a shrine. Another theory is that originally Unleavened Bread was only celebrated on the seventh day after Pesach, and that later the celebration was enlarged and extended backward to join it to Pesach. An ongoing problem with Pesach and Unleavened Bread ceremonies was that this was a prime time for harvesting and planting, so many would feel pressured to keep working the fields as much as possible.

23:9–14

Perhaps in ancient times individual farmers brought the first sheaves of barley harvest to local shrines, with some related sacrifices. The sheaves probably went to the priest. Later it seems that the shrine or temple provided everything, and the people did not have to travel at all. There would have been one set of animals sacrificed in the name of all. Another theory is that the offering of the sheaves might have overlapped at times with the trip for the Unleavened Bread ceremony.

23:15–22

This passage calls for a shrine offering fifty days later of the first sheaves of new wheat and related sacrifices. This seems to have been another event for which the shrine or temple eventually supplied everything. It was always a minor festival, despite coaxing about its importance by Priestly writers. Another theory is that the barley and wheat ceremonies were combined to start with.

As with the barley, all wheat did not ripen at the same time throughout the country; there was about a month's range in local conditions. The major danger near the time of wheat harvesting was dry Egyptian east winds, which could wither and devastate wheat right before harvesting.

23:23–25

The first day (new moon) of the seventh month was marked by trumpet blasts. This important feast was described in Num 29:1–6. Most new moon rites were minor, but this seventh month included the Day of Atonement (Yom Kippur) on the fifteenth, and then the eight-day harvest festival of Ingathering or Booths. The trumpets on the first day thus marked the entire month. In post-biblical traditions this seventh new moon became Rosh Hashanah, the new year festival.

This seventh month was the one quiet period at the end of the major harvests and before the new planting and rainy seasons would begin. It was the best time for a major harvest celebration.

In Lev 23:24 this first day is called a *day of complete rest* (*shabbaton*). It is related to the word *Sabbath* and means a *Sabbath-like day*. The term comes up again twice in 23:39. Apparently a *day* of complete rest was less rigid than *an actual Sabbath* of complete rest (23:3); more extensive food preparation was allowed.

Some scholars note that trumpet blasts were originally sounds of alarm. That original overtone might have persisted in this festival, if we take the alarm to be the call to everyone to pray for ideal harvesting conditions, followed by the needed rains at the end of the same month.

23:26–32

H borrows ancient ceremonial details about Yom Kippur from Num 29:7-11 and parts of Lev 16:29-34a. The Lev 23 style is grim, highlighting the punishments in 23:29-30. In 23:27 the word is actually plural, *atonements* (*hakkippurim*). This could be a form of intensification, meaning something like a *day of complete atonement*. Everyone's fasting will be a sign of unity and will make the high priest's confession of the nations sins all the more efficacious. The restriction on work is equally severe; it is called a *Sabbath of complete rest* (*shabbat shabbaton*) as in 23:3.

To call the Day of Atonement *your Sabbath* (23:32) is another way of personalizing the appeal to observe this special day. It could also be a way of continuing to give the highest honor to the goodness of creation—the seventh day of Genesis, when God rested on *his Sabbath*.

Milgrom takes this passage in Lev 23 as a shift in focus from cleansing the sanctuary to the cleansing of the people themselves.

23:33–43

The section on the harvest festival (much of Lev 23:33-43) was built on Num 29:12-38. In Lev 23:34 the *festival* (*hag*) is identified by the word *booths* (*succoth*). Normally the word *hag* is used for *pilgrimages*.

The only other pentateuchal uses of this phrase *hag succoth* are in Deut 16:13, 16; 31:10. Other instances are post-exilic. So Milgrom concludes that the term was used mainly when the festival was celebrated at the temple.

Booths (also called Ingathering, the old term in Exod 23:16; 34:22) was the main harvest and crop storage celebration of the entire year, occurring in the one-month window before the time for new planting and the rainy season. It was the best time to consider a week-long festival at Jerusalem. In later centuries, as farming gave way to herding endeavors, Passover became an equally practical time for many families to come and spend time in Jerusalem.

Lev 23:36 speaks of the *eighth day* as a *solemn assembly* (*aseret*), which most readers would consider the final day of the pilgrimage-festival. There are several technical points about this day that lead scholars to consider it to have been originally a completely separate holy day which had now been added onto Booths. *Solemn assemblies* were often town celebrations, and Milgrom suggests that this eighth day may have developed from special ceremonies where people prayed for successful harvests or, perhaps more likely, for rain at the start of the next planting season. That period of the year often had unstable weather—squalls, hail storms, locusts, or harsh dry winds.

23:37-38

These two verses serve as a conclusion to what precedes in Lev 23. Verse 37 echoes parts of 23:4, while the setting apart of Sabbaths and the gifts of individuals in 23:38 indicates that the conclusion is not in parallel with the emphasis on Sabbaths in 23:1-3. The phrase *Sabbaths of the LORD* in 23:38 refers in context to the regular animal sacrifices on those days. This is the only use of this phrase in the Old Testament, and offers another hint that in 23:2-3 the Sabbath is spoken of in nontraditional terms when it is called an appointed festival and a holy convocation.

23:39-43

This additional set of instructions for the festival of Booths has odd components. The phrase *festival* (*hag*) *of the LORD* occurs twice (23:39, 41), but the title *festival of booths* is not used, as it was in 23:34. The first and eighth days are called *days of complete rest* (*shabbaton*), but the title *holy convocation* of 23:35-36 is not used.

The gathering of tree branches and the rejoicing in 23:40, and the making of booths in 23:42, were not mentioned in 23:33–36. Lev 23:36 referred to a *solemn assembly*, without any details, whereas in 23:43 we are reminded that Israel lived in booths when they migrated from Egypt.

Milgrom takes 23:39b (the references to seven days, and to the two days of complete rest) and 23:42–43 (the mention of booths and the story of leaving Egypt) as modifications of older traditions.

In the older form the branches could simply have been waved about in processions around the altar in harvest celebrations at local shrines, and later at the temple. Later rabbinical commentary kept the memory of this waving alive. The rabbis were also aware of the use of these branches as signs of prayer for rain in the coming season. In Zechariah's visions of perpetual streams flowing from Jerusalem, and of a worldwide dominion by God himself, the prophet speaks of all the families of the earth coming to Jerusalem to worship at the annual festival of booths. He ends with the warning, "If any of the families of the earth do not go up to Jerusalem to worship the King, the LORD of hosts, there will be no rain upon them" (Zech 14:17).

At large pilgrimages to shrines or to the temple booths were quickly set up as needed by those who traveled from a distance, but they were simply temporary housing and not a deliberate recreation of imagined shelters used during the forty years of wandering in the desert. As Milgrom notes, any booths used at Passover would have been very temporary affairs, but ones used at Ingathering had to last for seven or eight days. A large number of these shelters spread out on the hills nearby could have been the signature image that gave a new name to an old festival.

We had mentioned earlier that 23:3 seems to be a late interpolation, and in these last few verses we have seen odd disparities in descriptions of the festival of booths. The likely explanation for some of these fine points could be the exile. During the exile the Holiness school tried to hold onto whatever they could from the stable routines of the temple. They could not have Sabbath animal sacrifices (or those for other holy days), but they could refrain from work under their control. They could eat unleavened bread at the appropriate time, fast on Yom Kippur, and perhaps share the joy associated with the harvest festival of Succoth, although there was no altar for the processions mentioned above. The old word for *pilgrimage festival* (*hag*) took on the more general meaning of *festival*, since there were no pilgrimages in Babylon.

The exiles also put more emphasis on circumcision, as another stable routine to help maintain their identity. They searched through the stories of Moses and his people being made to wander through the desert for their spiritual purification. Here were images of encouragement for the exiles as they went through their second captivity and desert experience near Babylon, a thousand miles from their true homeland. Even if Moses and the ancestors had actually lived in tents, the alternative notion of makeshift shelters from leaves and branches was easy enough for a later generation to imagine, as they lived under duress.

Many decades later, when the first exiles came back to Jerusalem, Ezra (Neh 8:13-18) and the other priests may have assumed that all the branches had been used to build booths in the period before the exile. Ezra also assumed that everyone should use booths from now on, even if they had to put them on the flat roofs of their small houses. When everyone uses the same symbol it becomes a badge or an icon of identity. Temporary booths are still used at Succoth in Jewish neighborhoods of major cities today, although the materials and styles of construction could be called ragtag. What's important is identity; plywood, canvas or plastic sheeting, dried cornstalks, or chain-link fence segments work just fine.

Conclusion

There may be four chronological levels of tradition in Lev 23. Milgrom divides them this way (with my simplifications).

- A. An old folk tradition in 23:10-14 describes the offering of first barley sheaves, most likely at a local shrine. The next sacrifice, of the first wheat sheaves, follows in 23:15-20. Milgrom assumes that the sheaves were offered by individuals at local shrines as crops matured at different times in different regions. Finally, 23:39-40 portrays some of the elements of the feast of Ingathering, including the use of branches in joyful processions. Ingathering was more likely at a fixed date, since it was a regional or national celebration.

- B. A later H refinement in 23:11, 15, 16 specifies that the sheaves had to be offered on the day after the Sabbath (Sunday in our system).

C. The bulk of the chapter is from Holiness editors, who focused on Jerusalem. The various new barley and wheat sacrifices of lambs, rams, goat, bulls, flour, oil, and wine reflect temple rituals rather than the offerings of individuals at local shrines. Individuals would never have been able to provide these quantities.

In 23:26–32 the various commands about fasting and abstaining from work at the Day of Atonement, as well as the penalties for not doing these things, seem to make more sense for a national ceremony based in Jerusalem. The term Booths (instead of Ingathering) in 23:34 could recall the pilgrims' booths when they came to Jerusalem, and the waving of branches is implied in 23:40.

D. A final H editor may well have added changes developed in the period of the exile. Avoiding work on the Sabbath is highlighted in 23:3, and the use of unleavened bread is stated again, along with the two days of abstaining from work and related sacrifices (23:6–8). Many prayers and practices from the Day of Atonement could still be shared in common. The extension of the obligation for all Israelites to construct booths, and the reference to booths used during the wilderness period (23:42–43), were additional elements of ritual that could have helped hold the exiles together.

Section Nineteen

Leviticus 24:1–23

Questions

92. Considering 24:5–9, what religious purpose do the twelve loaves serve before they are consumed by the priests?

93. Are there any unusual details in 24:10–12?

94. How stern is 24:13–16, 23? Can you imagine any problems in the use of this law in later generations?

95. Let us assume for the moment that 24:17–22 explains some legal parameters, and that the mention of specific injuries may well represent standards of proportion rather than actual injuries to be inflicted by court order. Why are these topics of capital punishment for murder and proportional standards for other cases in the same chapter as the account of a specific issue of blasphemy?

Leviticus 24 at first seems to be a catch-all chapter. The regulations about lamp oil and sanctuary loaves seem to have little connection with the questions of judging the man who blasphemed or the related rules about violence and murder.

The chapter may be outlined as follows:

24:1–4   The use of the oil for the lamp stand
24:5–9   The regular placing of loaves (and incense)
24:10–12 The case of the blasphemer

24:13-23   God's decisions about blasphemy, murder, and violence

Our first task will be to consider the lamp oil and loaves, which must be supplied by the people on a regular basis. These details can logically follow Lev 23, which focuses on the people's responsibility for the liturgical calendar.

In Israel, olive oil making was an extensive cottage industry. The purer the oil, the less soot it produced as fuel for lamps. The lamp burning through the night might also represent God's unfailing presence in the temple at all times. In neighboring cultures comparable use of lamps, incense and loaves may have been ancient representations of the fire, aroma, and food offerings made to gods.

Earlier commands about the oil are found in Exod 27:20-21 (which might be an insert from H). Centuries later Pharisees were able to have the lamp stand and the table with the loaves brought out from the temple for public view on certain pilgrimage festivals. It seems that they wanted to prove that the loaves were not meant as food for God. Another late temple custom developed in which the new loaves ready for use and the ones most recently removed were displayed temporarily in the outer court.

An older Priestly term, *presentation loaves* or *the bread of the Presence*, is used in Exod 25:30 and elsewhere. The Hebrew phrase is *lehem happanim*, meaning *bread for (God's) face* (or *person*). The term was avoided by later authors sensitive to anthropomorphisms.

As was just mentioned, many ancient Near Eastern groups placed various sorts of breads and special wine or beer in front of their idols. The drink offerings were poured out and the breads were burnt or exchanged for new ones daily. Apparently they were considered to be some sort of spiritualized food for the gods.

The main difference with our passage is that the loaves are exchanged just once a week, on the Sabbath. Given how long the loaves remained on the table, they could not have represented food in the same way as those put daily before idols. The twelve loaves were instead exposed or presented before God as a sign or reminder to him of his ongoing covenant relationship with the twelve tribes of Israel.

Lev 24:8 notes that Aaron "shall set them (the loaves) in order before the LORD regularly as a commitment of the people of Israel, as a covenant forever." The NRSV phrase *as a commitment of the people* is a

24:13–23   God's decisions about blasphemy, murder, and violence

Our first task will be to consider the lamp oil and loaves, which must be supplied by the people on a regular basis. These details can logically follow Lev 23, which focuses on the people's responsibility for the liturgical calendar.

In Israel, olive oil making was an extensive cottage industry. The purer the oil, the less soot it produced as fuel for lamps. The lamp burning through the night might also represent God's unfailing presence in the temple at all times. In neighboring cultures comparable use of lamps, incense and loaves may have been ancient representations of the fire, aroma, and food offerings made to gods.

Earlier commands about the oil are found in Exod 27:20–21 (which might be an insert from H). Centuries later Pharisees were able to have the lamp stand and the table with the loaves brought out from the temple for public view on certain pilgrimage festivals. It seems that they wanted to prove that the loaves were not meant as food for God. Another late temple custom developed in which the new loaves ready for use and the ones most recently removed were displayed temporarily in the outer court.

An older Priestly term, *presentation loaves* or *the bread of the Presence*, is used in Exod 25:30 and elsewhere. The Hebrew phrase is *lehem happanim*, meaning *bread for (God's) face* (or *person*). The term was avoided by later authors sensitive to anthropomorphisms.

As was just mentioned, many ancient Near Eastern groups placed various sorts of breads and special wine or beer in front of their idols. The drink offerings were poured out and the breads were burnt or exchanged for new ones daily. Apparently they were considered to be some sort of spiritualized food for the gods.

The main difference with our passage is that the loaves are exchanged just once a week, on the Sabbath. Given how long the loaves remained on the table, they could not have represented food in the same way as those put daily before idols. The twelve loaves were instead exposed or presented before God as a sign or reminder to him of his ongoing covenant relationship with the twelve tribes of Israel.

Lev 24:8 notes that Aaron "shall set them (the loaves) in order before the LORD regularly as a commitment of the people of Israel, as a covenant forever." The NRSV phrase *as a commitment of the people* is a

Section Nineteen

For Lev 24, Milgrom argues that Holiness editors inherited the entire passage—the narrative, the law about blasphemy, and the broader principle of *talion* (the *eye for an eye* image). The word *talion* is borrowed from the Latin *lex talionis* (principle of equality).

Milgrom assumes that all four cases—how to regulate those who blaspheme, the possibility of celebrating Passover a month later, the stern punishment for working on the Sabbath, and the complex matter of unmarried women inheriting—could well represent ancient problems that could reasonably have been portrayed retroactively as cases for Moses to consider.

Milgrom takes the time to present the entire passage in two outlines. The first is the classis chiastic structure, wherein we indent verses and phrases to see what ideas were duplicated and what should go in the center. The various parts are labeled in the standard manner, A-B-X-B'-A.' Our passage is complex, having a small center at the middle of 24:16 and a more important center at 24:20a. It is helpful to use the second outline also, where the two topics are put into columns—a shorter column for the blasphemy case and a longer column for the principle of *talion* in murder cases.

I include both outlines, keeping them each on own its page for easy review.

A	[13] The LORD spoke to Moses, saying:	
B	[14] Take the blasphemer outside the camp; and let all who were within hearing lay hands on his head, and let the whole congregation stone him.	
C	[15] And speak to the people of Israel, saying:	
D	Anyone who curses God will bear the sin.	
a	[16] One who blasphemes the name of the LORD shall be put to death;	
x	the whole congregation shall stone the blasphemer. Aliens as well as citizens,	
a'	when they blaspheme the Name, shall be put to death.	
E	[17] Anyone who kills a human being shall be put to death.	
F	[18] Anyone who kills an animal shall make restitution for it, life for life.	
G	[19] Anyone who maims another shall suffer the same injury in return:	
X	[20] Fracture for fracture, eye for eye, tooth for tooth;	
G'	the injury inflicted is the injury to be suffered.	
F'	[21] One who kills an animal shall make restitution for it;	
E'	but one who kills a human being shall be put to death.	
D'	[22] You shall have one law for the alien and the citizen; for I am the LORD your God.	
C'	[23] Moses spoke thus to the people of Israel;	
B'	and they took the blasphemer outside the camp, and they stoned him to death.	
A'	The people of Israel did as the LORD commanded Moses.	

Section Nineteen

Now the same passage in two columns.

(A) [13] The LORD spoke to Moses, saying:

(B) [14] Take the blasphemer outside the camp; and let all who were within hearing lay hands on his head, and let the whole congregation stone him.

(C) [15] And speak to the people of Israel, saying;

(D) Anyone who curses (his) God will bear the sin.	**(E)** [17] Anyone who kills a human being shall be put to death.
(a) [16] One who blasphemes the name of the LORD shall be put to death;	**(F)** [18] Anyone who kills an animal shall make restitution for it, life for life.
(x) the whole congregation shall stone the blasphemer. Aliens as well as citizens,	**(G)** [19] Anyone who maims another shall suffer the same injury in return:
(a') when they blaspheme the Name, shall be put to death.	**(X)** [20] Fracture for fracture, eye for eye, tooth for tooth;
	(G') the injury inflicted is the injury to be suffered.
	(F') [21] One who kills an animal shall make restitution for it;
	(E') but one who kills a human being shall be put to death.
	(D') [22] You shall have one law for the alien and for the citizen; for I am the LORD your God.

(C') [23] Moses spoke thus to the people of Israel;

(B') and they took the blasphemer outside the camp, and stoned him to death.

(A') The people of Israel did as the LORD commanded Moses.

A key point in our passage is that in 24:19-20 the phrase *give* or *be given* a *blemish* (*ntn mum*) is used. The NRSV translates to *maim* or to *inflict an injury* and to *suffer the (same) injury*. Blemishes of priests and sacrificial animals were featured in Lev 21–22, and there are many theological connections back to the blemishes against the moral law and justice in Lev 19 (see question 76 and the conclusion on Lev 19).

Here in Lev 24 the editors link blaspheming the name with harming the whole congregation. They rank blasphemy with murder and violence against humans. Earlier in Leviticus (10:1–7) the defiling of the sanctuary by Aaron's two sons was an unforgivable sin; so here blasphemy under certain circumstances also is considered unforgivable.

Presumably the blasphemer did not simply revile or ridicule God, but cursed God himself by name. He might have said something like "May God be damned." The seriousness of the insult attests to the deep-seated ancient concept that all curses have inherent power. Nowadays we would consider such verbal antics a complete waste of time; how can any creature harm a supreme being? But as Milgrom (2141) notes, for H anyone could blaspheme, even "a marginal, anonymous Israelite of questionable pedigree and dubious religious culture, let alone lack of genuine training, attacking YHWH in some unspecified part of the camp with the power of his human voice alone."

24:11–16

The actual case has its own complexities. The fracas began with one half-Israelite, half-Egyptian whose mother was from the tribe of Dan. Traditionally Danites were usually regarded as being too comfortable with mixed marriages and idolatrous superstitions. The man blasphemed *the Name*. This is a euphemism so that the name of the LORD is not dishonored in the very telling of the story. The man was put in temporary custody until decisions were made. The death penalty might have been a clear issue for full Israelites, but what should be done for one of mixed cultures, of for a resident alien? Moses had a right to be cautious.

In God's instructions to Moses all those who heard the curse must come forward. Milgrom argues that the laying on of hands is a sign of transfer of a pollution or desecration that befell the hearers. Now the desecration is removed from then and put back upon the perpetrator. Milgrom admits that this pollution or desecration of the hearers is not spelled out in biblical sources, but he considers it a reasonable inference. By contrast, the man who gathered wood on the Sabbath in Num 15 did not harm others in quite the same way, and his execution was simpler.

In 24:15 the Hebrew mentions any man "who curses *his* god." The NRSV modifies this to "who curses God," taking the larger story in context, and in line with some Septuagint manuscripts. Milgrom argues that we should consider the general statement in 24:15 and the specifically Jewish case in 24:16 as one legal standard. Some who curse a god or God will not be apprehended or not be proven guilty (perhaps they did not utter a divine name), but they "bear the sin" nevertheless. Divine punishment will follow in some fashion. But those who are publicly proven to have blasphemed the Name merit death, a death to be carried out by resident aliens as well as citizens. The resident aliens were equally harmed by the curse to start with. Aliens will be mentioned again in 24:22; this is another indicator of the unity of the entire passage.

Milgrom argues that just as 24:15–22 is a unified block, so 24:10–23 is also unified, reworking an old talion law into this narrative. Talion can be said to be the principle that punishment should be commensurate to the harm done—not greater in revenge, nor lesser in indulgence. This principle raises personal injuries from a civil tort to a criminal law, increasing the social worth of a citizen. But it is a principle, not a call to gouge exactly one eye or break exactly one ankle. No court could literally administer such a punishment; rabbinical commentators consistently called for compensation instead, except for capital cases.

Here the curse pollutes the community and endangers their very ability to live on the land, so the community virtually had to kill the blasphemer in self-defense.

Another point to keep in mind is that God's talion need not always be precise.

He punishes collectively, handing out either warnings or death. As Milgrom notes, "thus talion is frequently but a literary figure for the purpose of vividly emphasizing that God's justice is uncompromisingly inexorable" (2121).

24:17–22

The subject in 24:17 is *anyone* (*kol nefesh adam* = *any human being*). This very inclusive term certainly covers any non-Israelite living in the land.

The final phrase in 24:18, *life for life*, seems ill placed. Milgrom takes a guess that it might originally have followed *tooth for tooth* in 24:20. It does not appear at the parallel position (F') in 24:21.

The references to fracture, eye, and tooth in 24:20 are meant to be guidelines for the principle. In the same verse the Hebrew has "the blemish inflicted *on a person (adam)*." The NRSV does not translate the phrase *on a person*, relying on the context.

Lev 24:21 is an exact summary of 24:17–18, as part of the chiastic style. It also drives home the basic postulate that there can be no leniency for a rich person who takes a life; he or she cannot simply pay compensation.

The *one law* of 24:22 is an inclusive civil law, protecting the resident alien as well. The final second-person plural in *the LORD your God* is another indicator that resident aliens are involved; a singular form is usually used for references to Israelites alone.

The twinned subjects of blasphemy and talion in 24:13–23 are fully integrated. They are parts of one message from H. The heart of the message is the triple use of the word *blemish (mum)* in 24:19–20. (In the related citations in Exod 21:23–25 and Deut 19:21 the word *blemish* is not used.) So anyone who injures a person has blemished a person made in the image of God; we can take this as another form of blasphemy or desecration. As Milgrom notes, the law concerning the stoning of a blasphemer is subordinate to the major law in 24:24 that there should an equality of justice for murders, bodily injuries to humans, and the killing of another person's animals. Blasphemy is a direct offense against God, and all the more so are the killing or maiming of any of God's people, made in his image. The story of the blasphemer sets the stage for the greater law.

Perhaps principles like talion reflect a more secure society, giving maximum protection to free citizens and lessening differences between rich and poor. The rich can't buy their way out of violent crimes, and no one should receive excessive or multiple punishments for one event. The graphic phrases, such as *eye for eye*, were kept in biblical passages for emphasis.

Section Twenty

LEVITICUS 25:1–55

Questions

96. Judging just from 25:1–7, how or why should agricultural land get a Sabbath-year rest?
97. In 25:10–12 Jubilee years are set aside for people to return to their properties and to let the land lie fallow for another year beyond the Sabbath year. Is 25:10 self-explanatory?
98. How do 25:14 and 17 function along with 25:15–16?
99. How well does 25:18–22 illuminate 25:11–12?
100. What is the purpose of 25:23–24?
101. What is your first impression of the laws in 25:25–28, 35–43, 47–54?
102. Taking 25:29–34 and 25:44–46 as subunits, how do they relate to the rest of the chapter?
103. What is the purpose of 25: 23, 42, 55?

Lev 25 outlines customs for having farm fields lie fallow on a regular basis, and for allowing property to be returned to the original needy owner within a clan or tribe by the end of a set period. Commentators take this chapter to be close in spirit with Lev 19, so the two chapters promote the links between holiness and justice.

While the regulations are somewhat lengthy, they are fairly well organized. The chapter can be outlined as follows:

    25:1–7   A seventh-year rest for farm fields

25:8–12	Return of property at the end of fifty years (Jubilee)
25:13–17	Purchase prices set according to the Jubilee cycle
25:18–22	Reassurances that fallow periods will not cause famine
25:23–24	Recap of Jubilee system
25:25–28	The basic system for buying back a property
25:29–31	Short-term buying back for houses within walled cities
25:32–34	Special rules for properties in designated towns for Levites
25:35–38	Treating poor Israelites as resident aliens
25:39–43	Treating destitute Israelites as hired or bound laborers
25:44–46	Non-Israelites may be enslaved
25:47–55	Rules for Israelites in servitude to resident aliens

Milgrom notes that attempts to find differing literary sources for the various sections of the chapter do not enhance the task of appreciating the theology of the editors. He (2150) remarks, "The chapter, as is, flows logically and coherently. Even if the redactor had different sources before him, he welded them together in such an artistic and cogent sequence that it suffices to determine what he had in mind."

The main focus of the chapter is about land, except for the houses mentioned in 25:29–33. Some key phrases are used frequently: *property* (*ahuzza*, often meaning *land*), *redeem* (*gal*), *Jubilee* (*yobel*), and *Sabbath rest* for the land. Milgrom prefers to use *holding* for *property*, to remind us that various parcels of land are really being leased rather than sold in our sense of the word.

The explicit mention of Mt. Sinai in 25:1 is unusual, and the repetition of the same name in 26:46 probably serves as a clue to the importance attached to both chapters.

25:2–7

This first section opens with the statement that *the land* shall *observe a Sabbath*; the Hebrew has *the land shall rest (shbt) a Sabbath*. Usually the idiom is that God or humans celebrate the Sabbath. The *land* is the subject of this verb only in Lev 25:3, 4, 6; 26:34, 35; see the very end of Exod 31:16–17, where God *rested (shbt)* and *was refreshed (wynfsh)*. *Nefesh* is a noun meaning *throat, breath*, or *life*. The very rare verb form in Exod 31:17 means that God *caught his breath* or *recaptured his life's strength*. So the land's Sabbath for the Lord is imbued with his presence; the land is to be returned to its condition on the Sabbath of creation in honor of the LORD. Milgrom (2159) shares a quote from the theologian Jurgen Moltmann at this point: "The crown of creation is not the human being; it is the Sabbath. It is true that as the image of God, the human being has his special position in creation. But he stands together with all other heavenly and earthly beings in the same hymn of praise of God's glory, and in the enjoyment of God's Sabbath pleasure over creation."

We can assume that resident aliens also had to observe this custom of letting fields lie fallow, since the whole land is under this obligation.

The practical rotation of productive and fallow fields is here given an entirely theological rationale. Lev 25:2–7 follows up on Exod 23:10–11, but expands it considerably. In Exod 23 it seems that each farmer simply schedules rotations for his own fields, whereas in Lev 25 the entire nation apparently follows a unified timetable. Agriculturalists note that vineyards and olive groves cannot in fact be left untended for a year; they need much more maintenance than grain fields. Perhaps the original custom had only to do with grain, and the later mention of grapes and olives in Lev 25 is more symbolic than realistic.

Each seventh year is to be a *Sabbath of complete rest* for the land (*shabbat shabbaton*, as in Lev 23). The *aftergrowth (sepiah)* in 25:5 is the spontaneous crop that comes up during the fallow year, when there is no tilling and sowing. At times it is almost as abundant as a regular crop, although usually somewhat less so. In 25:6–7 this crop is expected to feed all the farmer's dependents, his livestock, and even neighboring wild animals! The dependents, slaves (non-Israelites), and hired and bound laborers (Israelites or non-Israelites) all live on the farmer's land, so he is responsible for them.

The redundant phrase *for food* at the end of 25:7 was understood by rabbis to mean that the aftergrowth was for immediate use but should not be put in storage, as were the yields in regular years.

The consistent rabbinic tradition is that providing some food for the poor and resident aliens is not covered by Lev 25:6–7. This might be a bit surprising, since the poor and aliens are mentioned in Exod 23:10–11 (two different regulations). They are also allowed to glean in regular harvest years in Lev 19:9–10; 23:22.

25:8–24

The bulk of Lev 25 turns to the system of Jubilee years. The idea of fifty years (seven sets of seven years plus one) may have been modeled on 23:15 (seven sets of seven days plus one) for the loaves and sacrifices each year at the time of new grain. The fiftieth year begins on Yom Kippur, the tenth day of the seventh month, indicating a fall harvest calendar. (Rosh Hashannah is on the first day of the same month.)

In 25:10 the *hallowing* (*qdsh*), the *proclamation* (*qra*) of *liberty* (*drwr*), and the term *Jubilee* (*yobel*) indicate that the Jubilee year is not on the same sacrosanct level or cycle as the Sabbath year of rest in 25:1–7. The word for *liberty* (*drwr*) primarily means *release* or *emancipation* of those under restraint; in this chapter the focus is on fellow Israelites.

We learn in 25:13 that the Jubilee year is another time to have the fields lie fallow; this ties the Jubilee year in some ways to Sabbath years and to the weekly Sabbath. The main feature of the year, however, is the returning of *properties* (*ahuzza*, land). As noted, H uses this word in 25:10, 13, 25, 27, 28, 33, 41, 45, 46 and frequently in Lev 27. In 25:45–46 non-Israelite slaves are called *property*.

In Deut 15:1–11 we have traditions about *debt release* every Sabbath year; in Lev 25:8–19 we have conditions about *land release* at the Jubilee. Milgrom thinks H takes debt release at Jubilee for granted in this context, since land return without debt release would be meaningless; there would be no money to get started again on the land. The fifty-year scale gives the creditor or redeemer time to gain some profit from his loan, unless he made the loan very close to an upcoming Jubilee year. Milgrom doubts that many creditors actually pitched in to help others; he points to later rabbinic references about a custom of provisos in some contracts, to the effect that a coming Jubilee year would not be invoked by either party.

Lev 25:14–17 reminds us of the math. The point is clear in 25:16 that it is a number of crops or harvests that is actually being sold, rather than the land itself.

It is not only the number of harvests but also the productive capacity of that acreage that must be considered. Prime fertile bottomland would be worth more, just as it is now.

The references to *selling* (*mkr*) and *buying* (*qnh*) among Israelites are, in context, really references to *leasing*.

The term *make a sale* in 25:14 is from the Hebrew *tmkru mimkar*, meaning when *you sell things that can be sold*. This might also be an indirect way of indicating leasing rather than the ordinary absolute sale of real estate in itself. In this case the *things that can be sold* are the crops. Lev 25:17 is an exhortation for this ethic, even if it was not a custom that could be enforced.

Lev 25:18–22 makes more sense in relation to a sabbatical year (following on 25:7). \ It is hard to see that a second consecutive fallow period (the forty-ninth and fiftieth harvest years) would actually work out, since aftergrowth is usually abundant or adequate for just the first year. Milgrom notes that grain and wine can be stored for a few years, and so can olive oil if it is worked into a paste with flour.

Storing reserves prior to a sabbatical year of fallow land might be a challenge; storing ahead for two years would be very difficult. Milgrom discusses various possibilities for sowing and harvesting periods immediately prior to and following such a Jubilee two-year period, and has his doubts that these traditional schemes were actually workable. He asks again if the whole image of a Jubilee year was not altogether utopian.

Lev 25:23–24 serves as the transition to the various cases of debt and redemption of property. It is balanced by the concluding statement in 25:38. The principle is that *land cannot be sold in perpetuity* (*lzmtt*). The final Hebrew word actually means that the *land may not be sold without the right of repurchase*. The land cannot be held for any time past the next Jubilee year. Milgrom prefers the translation *the land must not be sold beyond reclaim*, i.e., the seller cannot revoke the sale's implicit reclaim clause.

The reason for the principle is quite simple. God says, "The land is mine; with me you are but aliens and tenants." The land of Israel was originally given to them by lot (Num 33:50–56 and Josh 14–19), so the deed came from God, and can only be revoked by him. Calling them aliens (*gerim*) and tenants (*yithyashbim*) is a bold, ironic image. Israelites have the same relationship to God as their own resident aliens, day laborers, and bound laborers have to the Israelites. The phrase *with me* in 25:23 means *under my authority*. The same meaning can be seen in 25:35, 36, 40, 45.

In 25:24 *the land that you hold* or the *land of your possession* (*ahuzzatkem*) could include perimeter lands such as the Transjordan. Sellers are to provide for (the right and duty of) *redemption* (*gulla*) of the land. The verb behind this noun is *gal*, from which we get the participle *goel* (*redeemer*). So the following verses will cover some cases between Jubilees where a redeemer could help out.

We have other ancient Near Eastern examples of the previous owner of a tract of land having a first option to buy the property back when it is offered for sale, but the Jubilee system is notable in that a return is forced at a set time.

The redeemer can help keep the farm within the family and clan, but since he will return it at the Jubilee, in a way the clan becomes less important than the individual original owner. So wealthier clan members, in a position to redeem properties such at this, should not gradually get to own all of a clan's territory.

25:25–55

It might help to outline the following four cases for farmers in economic distress.

    A.   Lev 25:25–28 depicts an Israelite farmer who finds it necessary to sell part of his land to some Israelite outside of his clan. In doing so the farmer risks not only his land, but also ancestral burial grounds. Presumably the farmer made first offers to redeemers, who legally chose not to act or did not act in time, but now they are encouraged to make things right. A redeemer should buy the land from him or from the current owner, and at the Jubilee the redeemer will give it back at no cost to the original farmer. In the long run the redeemer will break even, but will not make a large profit.

        An appendix, 25:29–34, represents a later period when fewer Israelites lived on small farms. Those selling houses in walled cities had only one year to buy them back. City dwellers may have been more financially secure; they were probably not farmers subject to droughts, blights, etc. If this rule is an innovation, it may give some evidence for a historical basis for Jubilee customs. Houses in country villages or hamlets, or those owned by Levites, remained covered by Jubilee rules. Meadows in common surrounding Levitical towns were never to be sold.

B. Next, 25:35–38 describes an Israelite farmer failing with the land he still owns. He can offer the land as collateral to another Israelite in order to take out a no-interest loan. So he becomes a tenant farmer on his own former land. He may gradually work off the loan, but gets clear title back at the Jubilee. The key phrase in this paragraph is that this Israelite farmer and his family shall be considered *as though resident aliens*. True resident aliens (non-Israelites) could at some point become slaves, but Israelites treated *as though* resident aliens should never be enslaved.

C. Lev 25:39–43 indicates that if the Israelite farmer cannot work off the loan he and his family can become *as hired or bound laborers* (*cscir ctwshb*) to another Israelite. As resident hirelings they do receive wages and could conceivably slowly work off the debt. At the Jubilee the land is returned at no cost, with any remaining debt forgiven. The phrase in 25:39 that the man *sells himself* (or better, *is sold*) is being used figuratively. The man is in fact being hired for a fixed period; the sale is what we call a paper transaction. Costs are being moved on accounting sheets, such as tuition remissions or deductions from salaries for room and board.

Lev 25:39 says that *you shall not make them serve as slaves*. The Hebrew can be translated *you shall not enslave him with the slavery of a slave*. The vocabulary shows the author's disapproval of the very idea of enslaving an Israelite. The hired or bound laborer is a day worker, but he does not live in his own free home; he lives with his family on the landowner's property, something like United States migrant farm workers now who live in spartan bunkhouses or cabins provided by employers.

D. In 25:47–54 an impoverished Israelite farmer might come under debt to a non-Israelite. The NRSV describes such poor people as *selling themselves* to an alien. Milgrom argues that a better translation is that these poor people *are sold*. The verb form (*nmkr*) is passive, without identification of the subject. Keeping the phrase *are sold* avoids the wrong impression that a sale of self to a non-Israelite is voluntary or legitimate. In this case, a redeemer has the right to intervene and should intervene, buying the property. Then the farmer and his family would work for the redeemer until the Jubilee, when the land is to be returned. In some cases an impoverished farmer could save his wages and buy his freedom after many years.

If no redeemer comes forward, the Jubilee year system is still in effect, and whoever owns the land at that point must return the land at no cost. The point is that no Israelite should ever come under the fiscal control of a resident alien.

In the ancient Near East many slaves were originally freeborn native defaulting debtors and their children. Some were war captives or conquered serfs of other nationalities. The ideal that no Israelite should ever be enslaved may not have been achieved in practice. Milgrom notes frequent prophetic complaints about the treatment of slaves, although no prophet called for the abolition of all slavery. In 25:44–46 slavery is allowed in Israel, using foreign-born people sold to Israelites by foreigners, or using impoverished resident aliens and their children. Some of the resident aliens could have been of Canaanite background, or descendants of Canaanite marriages to foreigners. The phrase in 25:45 *you may acquire (qnh)* and its related noun *mqnh* can refer to any possession, be it slaves, fields, or cattle.

Given that Israelites treated as resident aliens or as hired bound laborers received the equivalent of interest-free loans or room and board at cost without any further profit surcharge, they had some chance of working off their debts; and the Jubilee would be the safety net in the last resort. Redeemers are not mentioned in the B and C cases above since they were called on to save land but not to remedy other sorts of debt.

In describing hired or bound laborers and their children in 25:41, 54, no mention is made of the wives of these laborers, the mothers of these children. Milgrom thinks that H in Lev 25 deliberately contradicts Exod 21:1–7, where wives could be enslaved and children held behind.

In Exod 21 there were Hebrew slaves, but they were to be freed after six years of service. There is no mention there of helping the newly freed slave to start over. In Deut 15:13–15 giving start-up money to a newly freed slave is encouraged but not demanded. In Exod 21:5–6 a slave could renounce his impending freedom, either to stay with the wife and children he would otherwise have to leave behind, or perhaps as a safer choice than starting over with no help at all.

By comparison, the situation in Leviticus 25 is a great improvement. An Israelite might work for several years to pay off much of his debt, but he was not actually reduced to the legal status of a slave. He could keep his family intact and receive his land back at the Jubilee year at the latest, putting him and his family in a realistic position to start over again.

The H editors of Leviticus do not even mention the freeing of Hebrew slaves, as found in Exod 21:1–11 or Deut 15:12–18. Perhaps the editors assume that those Israelites treated *as though* resident aliens or *as* hired or bound laborers, with their steady wages and the other components of this "safety net" provided by redeemers and the Jubilee system, were in a better position than those Israelites in the Exodus and Deuteronomy profiles.

Biblical Hebrew is a rich and complex language, despite its limited vocabulary. In Lev 25 the various words for *resident alien, tenant, day laborer*, and *bound laborer* can be consistently translated. But the words for *servant* and *slave* are one and the same (*ebed*). The basic root verb to *work* (*ybd*) can refer to physical labor, slave work, work as a servant, or work (liturgical service) at priestly duties in the temple. The English phrases "you shall not *make them serve* as *slaves*" (25:39), "they shall *serve* with you" (25:40), and "they are my *servants* . . . they shall not be sold as *slaves* are sold" (25:42) all use this specific verb and noun pair. We read in the final verse (25:55) that God says "to me the people of Israel are *servants*; they are my *servants* whom I brought out from the land of Egypt . . ."

The irony is that we must use different words in English. It would be jarring to read in 25:42 that "they are my *slaves* . . . they shall not be sold as slaves are sold," or in 25:55 that "to me the people of Israel are *slaves*; they are my *slaves* whom I brought out." In modern English we think of the utter inhumanity of slavery, whereas Old Testament (and New Testament) writers saw slavery as a natural part of a spectrum of service.

The best we can say is that God respects all honest human labor, although it has taken us many thousands of years to eliminate slavery, and in fact it still exists today under other guises.

Conclusion

The Jubilee customs in Leviticus 25 clearly called for the cancellation of debts and the restoration of lands. This might have been an old custom—pre-exilic or pre-monarchic—from a time when family membership and land ownership were practically the same thing. If such a custom were in place it could well have promoted or influenced many redemptions and terminations of debt even before the next Jubilee year came due.

Later on, land simply became one source of income among many, and absentee landlords foreclosed on small farmers down on their luck. At many points kings confiscated properties so they could run their own patronage systems. Prophets criticized the steady impoverishment of the lower classes.

Milgrom offers evidence that the system of having the land rest each Sabbath year was actually observed, perhaps more so after the exile. The matter of how well the Jubilee system was actually observed is harder to investigate. Milgrom notes that it was a moral law, but not judicially enforceable. However, the rules on houses in walled cities and Levitical towns seem to be realistic.

As we study these ancient biblical attempts to protect small farmers from insolvency, it is clear that not every part of the social network was subject to discussion. The status of resident aliens and non-Israelite slaves was a fact of life, even as moves were made to keep Israelites from becoming slaves themselves. Milgrom notes the clash between verses promoting civic equality, such as 19:33–34 or 24:22, and the strict tribal laws denying land ownership to any resident aliens. The latter had no network of redeemers or Jubilees, nor any possibility of such connections. Ezekiel briefly outlined an ideal future in which they could own land (Ezek 47:21–23), but did not get into practical details of redemption or Jubilee.

Section Twenty-One

LEVITICUS 26:1–46

Questions

104. Taking 26:1–2 as the beginning of a new section, how does it seem to be related to 26:3–13?
105. How would you characterize 26:3–13?
106. How would you characterize 26:14–39?
107. How would you characterize Lev 26:40–45?

Lev 26 uses elements of a solemn closing formula common to many ancient Near Eastern covenants and treaties: a medley of blessings and curses. The classic biblical instance is Deut 28:15–68.

In three places a few verses from an H source close to or during the time of the Babylonian exile have been woven into our chapter. Lev 26 can be easily outlined.

26:1–2	Introduction summarizing the Ten Commandments (late H)
26:3–13	Blessings
26:14–39	Curses (including 33b–35 from late H)
26:40–45	Remorse and recall of covenant (including 26:43–44 from late H)
26:46	Summary, linking all of Lev 25–26

As we shall see, the late H verses depict the holy land being deserted, with many Israelites in exile near Babylon. The message is that eventually atonement can be made, and then God can revitalize his covenant with Israel.

We can also look at 26:43-45 as the parallel to 26:1-2, in that 26:43-45 links the exile to the disobedience of Israel to God's laws and rules, and speaks of reactivating the Sinai covenant. In a way, 26:3-45 spells out the conditions for survival or destruction intrinsic to covenant theology.

There are several points of unity between Lev 25 and Lev 26. Lev 25:38, 42, 55 and 26:13, 45 refer to deliverance from Egypt. Sabbatical years are mentioned in 25:1-7 and 26:34-35, 43a. The main theme in both chapters is that violating God's commandments, especially the Sabbath laws, will lead to exile. Another parallel is that just as Israelites can redeem land for their poorer kindred, so God can redeem Israel from exile (26:39-45), if they repent of their ways.

The first two verses seem to be a medley of phrases from the First, Second, and Fourth Commandments; they can be taken to represent all Ten Commandments. This introduction (26:1-2) could also be considered a way of linking Lev 26 to the ethical content of Lev 19. A somewhat similar (although much longer) medley of practicalities can be found in Neh 10:30-39.

Concerns about idolatry and weekly Sabbath observations gradually became more prominent in some sections of the Pentateuch and in several of the prophets in the century before we come to the period of the exile. The weekly Sabbaths mentioned in Lev 26:2 may also be taken to include the Sabbath year system for letting fields lie fallow (every seventh year). By the same token, 26:33b-35, 43-44, which speak of Sabbath years, could also be taken to include weekly Sabbaths within those purviews.

In 26:1 the word for *idols* (*elilim*) is rare, appearing elsewhere only in 19:4. This could be another indicator that H wants us to link the contents of Lev 19 and Lev 26 together.

Carved images (*pesel*) and simple *pillars* (*masseba*) at one time may have been legitimately used to represent God himself rather than other deities, but they had been long condemned. The *figured stones* or *pavement* (*eben maskit*) may be mosaic pictures on floors. The verb in Lev 26:1 for *worshipping* (*hwh*) may be meant to combine the essence of the phrases for *worshipping* and *serving* in Exod 20:5.

Lev 26:2 is quite close in wording to 19:30, and could refer to not working the land on weekly Sabbaths and during Sabbath years. We need to reverence God's times, as well as his sanctuaries.

26:3–13

The blessings here are really promises, and the curses to follow are really threats. Ezekiel borrows many phrases from Lev 26 (see Ezek 34:25–28; 37:26–27).

We can divide this section into five sets of blessings

26:3	Introduction
26:4–5	Abundance
26:6	Peace within the land
26:7–8	Victory over foreign enemies
26:9–10	Abundant life, fulfillment of the covenant
26:11–12	God's presence in Israel
26:13	God's self-declaration

The opening, 26:3, could refer to all of Lev 17–26, which H composed, and even to Lev 1–16, which is P material that H edited. Some stylistic points can be noted. For example, 26:4–5 is exhortatory, even poetic. It imitates 25:18–19, which has a more matter-of-fact or legal tone, because of its own context.

Milgrom suggests that the phrase for *maintaining* the covenant in 26:9 (*qwm berit*) is an important nuance from the basic meaning of the verb, which is to *establish* or *construct*. In Gen 17:7, 19, 21, for example, the covenant *established* in Gen 17:2 is being *maintained*. The same logic can be found in Ezek 16:60, 62 and Deut 8:18.

26:11–12

The reference to God establishing his *dwelling* in 26:11 means that he will now be present among them again. Though he never discarded his covenant, he had left them to their own sinful devices, withholding his presence, so to speak.

One could take the word *dwelling* to mean *presence*. Given that the blessings, curses, promises, and admonitions are cast in the future (when Moses was speaking, the tabernacle was in use), Milgrom argues that we should think of the *dwelling* (*mishkan*) as an ethereal, spatially unbounded *presence*. Ezekiel often uses the same word in this way (see Ezek 37:27-28 and 2 Sam 7:6). The point is that God will move about the whole land, from shrine to shrine.

The latter part of 26:11, *I shall not abhor you*, is a bit more graphic in the Hebrew (*my gullet shall not expel you*). The same image is used in curses in 26:15, 30, and in the references to the exile in 26:43-44. We should take it in a positive sense here and in 26:44. Even if Israel abhors God's commandments (26:43), God is ready not to loath Israel (26:44), awaiting only their repentance (26:40-42).

The rare phrase in Lev 26:12, *I will walk among you*, is found in Ezek 19:6; 28:14. It means to *walk to and fro*, as in Gen 3:8, when God walked in the garden of Eden. It is used quite often in later passages in Genesis (5:24; 6:9; 17:1; 24:40; 48:15). The divine promise in Lev 26:12 to *be your God* could also be translated as *I will continue to be your God*.

Milgrom notes that 26:11-12 is the only blessing not reversed in any of the curse formulae to follow.

The closing self-declaration is from the Sinai covenant story in Exodus. God, who rescued them from Egypt, has the power to shower down any blessings he wishes.

26:14-39

The litany of curses is quite harsh. We can see several subdivisions by content, as follows.

26:14-15   Introduction

26:16-17   Illness, famine, defeat

26:18-20   Drought, poor harvests

26:21-22   Harmful beasts

26:23-26   War, pestilence, famine

26:27-39   God abandons his shrines and land, and pursues Israel in exile

The phrases that introduce each set of curses make it clear that God is reacting to sinful stubbornness. He begins by matching punishment to sin, following the *lex talionis*, eye for eye, wound for wound. We find *I in turn* (the Hebrew has *I also*) in 26:16, 28. The verb *continue* (*ysp*) is used in *continue to punish* (18) and in *continue to plague* (21). We have the idiom that the people *continue hostile* (the Hebrew is *hlk qri, walk contrary*) in 26:21, 23, 27. In 26:24, 28 God reacts in the same way and *continues hostile* to them.

26:14–26

Lev 26:14 is a counterpart to 26:3. Some of the language in 26:14–15 is dramatic or emotional, but not specific; thus the references to *not obeying God*, *spurning* statutes, *abhorring* ordinances, *not observing* all the commandments. The *abhorring* of ordinances is the counterpart to the phrase about *abhorring* in 26:11 (*my gullet shall not expel you*). The covenant mentioned in 26:15 is most likely that of Sinai, and is in contrast to 26:9, where God maintains his part of the Sinai covenant.

In 26:17, *I will set my face against you* is the opposite of 26:9, *I will look with favor upon you* (the Hebrew is *I will set my face toward you*).

The word to *punish* (*ysr*) is a common verb in Wisdom books. There it means to *discipline*, to *administer corrective punishments*, as a parent might have to do at times to prevent a child from becoming truly spoiled (see Deut 8:5; 2 Sam 7:14; 2 Macc 10:4; 6:12–17; the last of these is moving). The author thanks God for punishing his people early and often, so that they can get back on the right track; otherwise we might go so far astray as to be lost forever.

In 26:13 God *broke* the Egyptian yoke on his people; in 26:19 God *breaks* the sinful pride of his own people. In 26:6 God removes dangerous beasts; in 26:22 he sends the same beasts back to attack flocks and people alike. In 26:6 there will be no *sword*, no invasion of the land; in 26:25, 33 God will send *swords*. In 26:25 there will be *vengeance for the* (Sinai) *covenant*, which Israel had broken in 26:15.

26:27–39

In the long grand finale of the curse section, God abandons his shrines and land, and pursues Israel in exile. In 26:28 he *continues hostile in fury* (*hmh qeri, the fury of hostility* or *opposition*), and will *punish* (*ysr*, the Wisdom word for *discipline*) sevenfold. Milgrom admits that here God is not calm, and is not following the *lex talionis*. God is impulsively imposing punishments, albeit with justification.

The *high places* of 26:30 were likely pagan shrines, while the *sanctuaries* of 26:31 were the various centers for the worship of God. God will devastate the land and leave it desolate in that he will expel the Israelites from it. Those outsiders who occupy it in their stead may find it adequate for their own needs.

The latter part of 26:33 introduces a new remark about the land being *desolate*. The interpolation continues in 26:34–35. Since the tradition of letting the land rest every seventh year had not been faithfully observed, the land will now *enjoy its Sabbath years* while the Israelites are in exile. Milgrom prefers to translate that the land shall be *paid its Sabbath years*. The NRSV and Milgrom simply use two variants of the same root form, *rzh*, meaning *enjoy* or *pay*.

The phrase *you shall perish*, found in 26:38, could be taken as *you shall be lost*, according to Milgrom. He prefers this translation because there are survivors, mentioned in 26:39–45.

Milgrom notes that H believes in vertical punishment from God down through the generations. During the exile expiation could not be properly sanctioned by sacrifices, so H accepts the fact that remorse and confession alone were available.

Later prophets like Jeremia and Ezekiel had less concern for collective sacrifices or confessions, and put more focus on individual repentance and God's unbounded mercy. Some of those prophets, especially Ezekiel, move away from this view of punishment down the generations. See Ezek 24:23, where the prophet quotes just part of Lev 26:39, "you who survive shall *languish* (*mqq*)" (in Ezekiel the NRSV has *you shall pine away in your iniquities*). The verb *mqq* can mean to *languish* or *waste away*, but it is a strong word and can also mean to *rot* or *putrefy*. When Ezekiel cites these words he is speaking of individuals suffering for their own sins, while the full verse in Lev 26:39 is that "those of you who survive shall languish in the land of your enemies because of *their* iniquities; also they shall languish because of the iniquities of their ancestors."

26:40–45

The chapter ends on a more positive note. Lev 26:40–41b allows for Israel to make a communal confession of their own sins and the sins of their ancestors. This must include their admission that they had remained hostile to God, so that he had to remain hostile to them and send them off into exile. A somewhat similar scene unfolds in Deut 30:1–10, following the graphic curses in Deut 28:15–68.

Should they make this confession, God's response (Lev 26:41b–45) will be to accept this confession as expiation or atonement, and restore them to their land as soon as the land has recovered from its neglected sabbatical years. The mention of the sabbatical years in 26:43–44 is also from the late H source, since it clearly speaks of the exile.

In 26:41 the people *make amends* (*rzh*) for their iniquity. Milgrom argues that this verb should always be translated in the passive sense, so we should say that the people *accept their punishment in full*. The confession is all that God requests. From that point all the activity comes from him; once the land has recovered from the damage of lost (neglected) sabbatical years, God will recall his covenant and restore them to their land (see Isa 40:2, "Speak tenderly to Jerusalem and cry to her that she has served her term, that her penalty is paid, that she has received from the LORD's hand double for all her sins").

The major part of the response by God starts in 26:42. The covenants with Jacob, Isaac, and Abraham are mentioned; Abraham's was the most important. Since the speaker (God) is casting his eyes ahead to the exile, we can assume that the writer also had the Sinai covenant in mind. The final phrase, *I will remember the land*, fits the context well, since the covenants with the patriarchs focused on the promise of land. In 26:43 we again have the image that the land will *enjoy* its Sabbath years (or *be paid* its Sabbath years, following Milgrom's suggestion). In the same verse the people *make amends* (or *accept their punishment in full*, as Milgrom had in 26:41). In 26:44 we have God's firm promise not to give up entirely on those in exile; he will not break his (Sinai) covenant with them under any circumstances, even though the Israelites had failed in 26:15.

The general term *ancestors* (*roshnim*), instead of *fathers*, in 26:45 could be another hint that the Sinai covenant is being considered here; perhaps it is a reference to the *mixed crowd* that went with them on the Exodus. While the NRSV uses the word *ancestors* in 26:39–40, the Hebrew has *fathers* in those two verses, likely focusing on the patriarchs. The writer is having God look back at much of Israel's history, losing sight of the fact that the escape from Egypt happened so recently.

All covenants have conditions, explicit or implicit. While we often think of the covenant with Abraham as an unconditional set of promises, Gen 18:17-19 shows God debating what to tell Abraham about Sodom. Finally, God decides to discuss this with Abraham: "... for I have chosen him, so that he may charge his children and his household after him to keep the way of the LORD by doing righteousness and justice; so that the LORD may bring about for Abraham what he has promised him."

God's bringing the people out of Egypt highlights Lev 26:13 as well as 26:45. So the blessings (26:3-13), and the curses (26:14-39), when they lead to a communal confession, end on the same hopeful note—that God will reconcile and rebuild his covenant people, whom he punishes but never abandons.

We could say that the exile can work like the flood at the time of Noah; both events can in some sense remove sin from the land.

Conclusion

Milgrom takes most of Lev 26 as being from eighth-century BCE traditions, with the few late H interpolations we have mentioned in 26:1-2, 33b-35, 43-44. He (2289) considers the curses from God to be given "only with reluctance. This chapter ... ends with consolation and hope that the punishment and confession will atone, based on the assumption that the covenant is eternal (vv. 40-45)."

Milgrom notes that the passage in Deut 30:1-10, while being a message of hope in the vein of Lev 26:40-45, puts more emphasis on repentance. In Deut 30 the people are called on to *return* (*swb*) to God (30:2, 10) by their actions. The tone in Deut 30 is more demanding than that of Lev 26:40-45, with its more generic call for confession, humility, and amends. Milgrom argues that the passage in Lev 26 is simply an older approach to the subject.

I find Milgrom's distinctions between Deut 30 and Lev 26 helpful, mainly to assist our analysis of Lev 26. To speak of two approaches to the topic of repentance reminds me of the traditional dry Catholic distinction between *imperfect* and *perfect* levels of contrition. Fortunately for all of us, Jewish and Christian alike, God brings more people home than we can imagine.

Section Twenty-Two

Leviticus 27:1–34

The final chapter concerns itself with various customs for making voluntary donations to the support of the temple and its officials. While some consider it an odd appendix for the entire book of Leviticus, one could make plausible guesses as to why editors may have thought it an appropriate way to end the book.

It may be that the contents of Lev 27 are older P regulations, but later H editors near the time of the exile may have placed them at the end of the book for two reasons. First, we could consider Lev 25 and 27 to flank 26. Lev 25, with the system of Sabbath years and Jubilees, calls on the more fortunate to *redeem* properties and assist their clansmen. Lev 27 allows for the *redemption* of some purchased lands, even though they had been devoted to the sanctuary. Amid the curses and blessings of Lev 26, there is hope at the end, hope that with Israel's repentance God will uphold the covenant and protect his people. So God's mercy is the paradigm for the call to mercy in the two adjoining chapters.

Secondly, we can see how Lev 27 complements Lev 1. The first chapter began with detailed instructions for the ordinary animal sacrifices at the altar. In the final chapter special explicit vows provide another way for people to support the complex needs of the temple, with its goal to assist everyone in worshipping the LORD.

Note that these voluntary donations were never meant to be the complete temple revenue stream. A regular annual tax of some sort was needed, in addition to careful management of those same funds.

Leviticus 27 can be subdivided as follows.

27:1–8	Donations vowed on a sliding scale based on the worth of slaves
27:9–13	Donations of extra animals
27:14–25	Donations of houses and fields
27:26–27	Donations of firstlings
27:28–29	Things devoted to destruction
27:30–33	New rules on tithing
27:34	Concluding sentence for entire book

Some of the customs are not that self-explanatory. *Making explicit vows* (*pla ndr*) to make donations related to the *estimated value* (*yrk*) of male or female slaves of this or that age group is not the same thing as donating slaves. Some commentators wonder if slaves had actually been donated in earlier times, but we have no proof for this. 2 Kgs 12:4 may refer to such donations of estimated values.

The fixed scale of shekels points to the significant worth of women slaves. They were least valuable during their childbearing years, which would make sense because of their burdens in bearing and rearing children. But they were more valued in their old age (40 percent). Milgrom notes that rabbis admitted that old men weren't of much use at household chores, compared with old women. It might not be too hard to find wives who think the same way today.

Lev 27:8 allows for priests to lower the fixed shekel scale for persons who wanted to make these explicit vows but were not wealthy enough to meet the costs called for in this law. Rabbis also issued guidelines so that these donations did no financial harm to the one making the vow or to any of the family.

When donating extra animals, there are rules that warn one not to *exchange* or *replace* a species (*hlp*) after making such a vow, nor to *substitute* (*mwr*) another of the same species. The latter verb appears three times in 27:33, where one should not *substitute* one animal for another when tithing from flocks.

Unclean animals, not eligible for sacrifice, are evaluated for their equivalent in money. The final verse, 27:13, is meant to discourage the one vowing from changing his mind and asking to buy back the animal in question. A fine of 20 percent is added in these cases, precisely to avoid the bother of having to sell back things already donated.

Lev 27:14–15 covers the donation of houses, with the same 20 percent fine to avoid having to sell something back to the donor.

Lev 27:16–21 focuses on donating one's *inherited landholdings* (*sdh ahz*). Given the instructions about adjusting the value by the Jubilee system, the donation amounts to giving a certain number of harvests (usufruct) until the point of redemption or the next Jubilee year.

The mention of the *seed requirement* in 27:16 indicates the average amount of seed grain needed to sow a given plot of land. This counting system works just as well as trying to compute square yards or acres of farmland. The rate of fifty shekels to a homer of grain seems to be the value of the crops for the whole fifty-year Jubilee period.

If not redeemed by the time of the Jubilee, the land goes to the sanctuary (the priest being its representative). This system prevents land donated to the sanctuary from immediately enriching religious officials; they only get the usufruct until the next Jubilee, and redeemers have plenty of time to intervene, if they can. The one difference here is that the original donor does not regain the unredeemed land at the Jubilee, unlike the poorer farmers forced to sell land in their need.

This system of checks and balances was probably meant to keep the temple from amassing vast wealth, as we see in Egypt, where the major temple priesthoods became an empire within an empire.

Lev 27:22 allows for donations to the sanctuary of *purchased lands* (not *inherited landholdings*). In these cases the original purchaser regains the land at the Jubilee.

In the H traditions the *firstling* (*becor*) of Lev 27:26 belongs to the LORD by definition. In Exodus and Deuteronomy firstlings must undergo consecration ceremonies instead. Milgrom takes the change in Leviticus to be deliberate. Lev 27 allows the sanctuary to profit from these animals, as well as from the sale of unclean animals.

The Hebrew of 27:28–29 uses forms of the noun and verb root *hrm*, which means to *ban* or *reclassify something entirely*. An indirect way of touching on the same custom was to speak of *declaring something most holy* or *dedicating it to God*. We know the phrases mainly from instances of holy war in Israel and other cultures, where captives taken in battle as well as booty were often destroyed.

Here the regulations seem to refer to times of peace, but we do not have many biblical parallels to study. There is a sketchy reference in Ezra 10:8 to property being *forfeited* (*hrm*) by those unwilling to divorce their Gentile wives. It is possible that those properties went to the temple. However, in Lev 27:28 the donor is the one who declares his own property to be banned or devoted. The pure animals must be used in whole burnt sacrifices (they may have been left to graze on meadows owned by the temple till needed). It seems that impure animals and other devoted property or slaves could be put to use as ordinary corporate assets of the temple.

The reference in 27:29 to humans being executed is puzzling. Milgrom reviews and discounts traditional rabbinic explanations that claim this death penalty was never carried out or that substitute penalties were allowed. He concludes that the legal executions in Lev 27 must have been authorized by court hearings, although we have no details.

Lev 27:30–33 speaks of tithing in general, as though it were an established custom. In many parts of the ancient Near East extensive tithes were often part of a royal tax system. In some cases the taxes were collected and administered by temple staff, who stored the goods and managed the livestock. Our Old Testament references to such tithes present an inconsistent picture of how regularly the tithing procedure was used and what was collected.

In Lev 27 the tithing from produce may have been for the benefit of the Levites, who had less income than the priests. The tithing from flocks is mentioned only here, and nowhere else in the Bible. Milgrom (2398) argues that the custom "may have been practiced voluntarily by well-to-do ranchers, but never became a universal and annual mandatory obligation followed by all of Israel."

Final Overview

Years ago I used to show parts of a documentary film series in a college course on various world religions. One visual segment remains clear in my memory. It was an annual Buddhist ceremony where all the villagers brought gifts for the monks of their monastery. The monks sat at one end of the plaza and, starting at the far end, all the gifts were solemnly passed up and down the rows of the people (also sitting) so that each and every adult got to touch each and every gift (mostly lengths of white silk, wrapped in special paper) before the gifts came up to the monks themselves. There were two reasons for this brigade formation: the poorest people who could not give gifts were not singled out, and everyone gained some spiritual merit in actually handling the gifts and passing them on.

There is a similar logic within Leviticus. All the rules for the various ceremonies and law cases are made known to all the people, not just to the priests or leaders who will carry them out. Everyone learns the whole system, so everyone is involved and empowered, just as all the Buddhist villagers were involved.

For anyone wishing to reflect on the theological impact of the entire book of Leviticus, it is clear that the editors had their own way of blending the more timeless or permanent elements of their worship system along with what we might call supporting, particular details. Other chapters, mixed among those elements, remind us more directly about our human sinfulness and limitations.

One can see the timeless elements in chs. 1–3 (whole burnt, grain, and well-being offerings), chs. 8–9 (the first ordinations and initial sacrifices), chs. 11–12 (clean and unclean foods, purifications after childbirth), chs. 16–17 (Yom Kippur and proper disposal of animal blood by everyone), ch. 21 (strict code of conduct for priests), ch. 23 (annual liturgical calendar), ch. 25 (sabbatical and Jubilee years), and ch. 26 (the great scene of blessings

Final Overview

and curses). Within this list one could take the description of Yom Kippur and the blessings and curses as the two high points.

I think we could list as supporting or particular details the topic of who may eat what segments of sacrifices, as found in 6:8–7:38. The rules and following complex discussion between Moses and Aaron in 10:8–20, and the specific procedures for skin eruptions and bodily discharges in chs. 13–15, could be listed here; so too the fine details in ch. 22 and the rules about donations at the end (ch. 27).

The interspersed theme of our own sinfulness and limitations arises in several places. Lev 4:1–6:7 includes expiation offerings for unintentional sins, failure to testify in law cases, becoming unclean or making rash oaths, and more direct injustices that require guilt offerings. The opening of ch. 10 shows God punishing the sacrilege committed by two of Aaron's sons, and the import of the Yom Kippur whole burnt sacrifices and banishment of the scapegoat (ch. 16) is all about our sinfulness before God most holy. Chs. 18 and 20 mention sexual temptations and failings as well as the horrifying topic of infant sacrifice, and ch. 24 brings up the case of the blasphemer and dire warnings about the desecration that murder brings to all of creation. The range of curses in ch. 26 arises from the deep-rooted stubbornness to which we all can cling.

As the editors and redactors weave together these various elements of our worship and our sinfulness, they seem to be both unquestioningly devout and quite realistic about life at the same time. Perhaps we can add chs. 10 and 19 to the two high points of the book already mentioned (Yom Kippur and the blessings and curses). In ch. 10 Moses forcefully directs Aaron and his surviving sons to perform their duties without mourning, although he does grant Aaron some leeway at the end.

The Utopia of Holiness in ch. 19 includes high ideals of right worship and blunt condemnations of idolatry and injustice. To remove the condemnations would be to ruin the kaleidoscopic effect of that whole chapter.

I think it is important for all of us to continue to contemplate the worth of Lev 19. The apparent jumble of laws, condemnations, and ideals in that chapter contribute to a noble tapestry, a vivid profile of faith and justice intertwined. Individual verses such as "You shall not hate in your heart anyone of your kin; you shall reprove your neighbor, or you will incur guilt yourself" and "The alien who resides with you shall be to you as the citizen among you; you shall love the alien as yourself" show us all how much God wants everyday life to be part of our moral journey.

The theme of mercy in 26:40–45 is noteworthy, as mentioned in Section Twenty-One and in Answer 107. God does not want to destroy everyone; he does not want to terminate the covenant this way. He wants to reconcile and rebuild, to give extra chances, to punish when needed but not to abandon.

I think the ease with which the P and H schools and editors combined all the timeless details of offerings with such a realistic awareness of how unworthy and defiant God's chosen people can become stems from their innate sense of corporate covenant spirituality. As the people of the covenants at Sinai, everyone shares in rituals of faith at home and at the shrine or tabernacle; everyone honors the proper food and eligibility regulations; and everyone is called to uphold the common code of justice. Likewise, everyone knows at least the temptation to shirk religious duties; everyone understands the lure of trying to contact other gods, ones more lenient or at least easier to understand; and everyone looks the other way at failings in marital life and thinks about the quick but dishonest chance to get a bigger slice of the pie. The covenants at Sinai were not a deal made by a people well on the way to sainthood; they were a cry for help from sinners who had hit bottom—a cry for help that they had not earned. The same is true for us believers even now.

In Numbers I think reflecting on the image of Aaron swinging a censer (Num 16:45–50) is a valid way to summarize that entire book. Raising the incense smoke was just one transitory act of atonement, one pause within a nightmare of belief and unbelief during those forty years.

Here in Leviticus I look back at the rites of Yom Kippur in ch. 16, especially the experiences of the high priest and the attendant who took the scapegoat away to the wilderness. As I mentioned in Answer 54 both men had specific, solitary duties. The high priest had to enter the holy of holies alone, and the one attendant spent several hours alone on his journey with the doomed scapegoat. Each set of duties was for the sake of the entire nation, and each of the two men needed to have an undivided heart in order to embody the repentance of all before the most holy God. We need undivided hearts also.

Wandering in the desert for forty years (or, centuries later, enduring exile for decades) was not a "black hole" of history. In Leviticus it is an arena within which we, like Moses and his people, can develop a deeper corporate relationship with a merciful but moral and just and challenging God.

Answers

Section One: Leviticus 1:1–17

1. Scholars offer several suggestions for the logic behind this form of worship. Since a great deal of the animal's mass is turned to gases and smoke by the fire, perhaps it was thought to be transferred or transformed to a more spiritual realm or state. The offering could be a tribute, and its relative cost could attest to the dedication of the worshipper.

Without coming to a firm answer as to the inner logic of holocausts, we must remember that a liturgical action is self-justifying, even if later generations of believers move on to different methods. Obviously Jewish people no longer perform any of these sacrifices. Likewise some early Christians shared in complete meals at their worship, in addition to the elements of bread and wine. This ceremony using an entire meal no longer obtains, but Christians are satisfied with their current eucharistic rites.

2. As we read about the burning of the cattle, sheep or goats, it is clear that the offerers and the priests are cooperating in the greater task. The gifts are voluntary; the offerer himself proclaims ownership of the animal and the intention to offer this particular sacrifice. The offerer is involved in extensive preparations—slaughtering, flaying, cleaning, and quartering the animal. The priests alone put the blood around the base of the altar, and perform the rituals that involve the fire and the altar itself. The smaller alternative offerings of birds, flour, or prepared breads may involve less effort all around, but are of equal worth in God's eyes.

Section Two: Leviticus 2:1–16

3. The grain offerings are similar to the whole burnt offerings of Lev 1, insofar as they are also freewill offerings. From our broader understanding

Answers

of Judaism we can assume that the grain offerings fulfill the same spiritual purposes as those in Lev 1, even though only token fractions are consumed by fire. The use of oil and frankincense, and the prohibition against burning any leavened bread, may hint at older customs where grain offerings had been totally burnt.

Priestly editors do not explain points of history or development in ceremonies; they simply present current practice as God's will. In this case there may have been religious reasons for assigning most of the grain offerings to the priests. A religious reason, such as countering an idolatrous or superstitious error, would make more sense than simply thinking of the bread as compensation for the priests.

Section Three: Leviticus 3:1–17

4. The great majority of the chapter consists of clear instructions, even if they are somewhat repetitious. Most readers would probably miss the supplementary obligation to have these sacrifices at shrines in 3:16–17.

The chapter offers no explanation for why the burning of sections of suet and other organs is an acceptable form of worship. It also does not profile the clan or extended family feasts that followed the ceremony. Scholars assume that feasts of this magnitude, where peasant shepherds or farmers would prepare meat from their herds or flocks, were rare occasions. Whatever the reason for the event, combining the sacrifice to God of the suet and certain organs, along with praise to him for blessings received, puts the focus on God's love for all his people.

In our own culture even national quasi-religious celebrations such as Thanksgiving or the Fourth of July usually derive their energy from family reunions rather than from the communal dimensions for which they are named. Perhaps the people whom Leviticus describes had more of a balance.

Section Four: Leviticus 4:1–35

5. Perhaps the blood is sanctified by sprinkling some of it toward the curtain shielding the ark. Then putting some blood on the horns of the two altars purifies the entire sanctuary. Burning the suet and designated organs could represent the entire animal offered in worship and in expiation. Having the rest of the animal incinerated at a distance from the

Answers

sanctuary is quite unusual; perhaps it is a sign of caution or danger. This burning of most of the bull is not a parallel to the use of the red heifer for ashes of purification, nor is it like the scapegoat driven into the wilderness at Yom Kippur.

6. In 4:15 elders lay hands on the animal, so representing the entire congregation. Lev 4:14 indicates that somehow the sin has been made known to the people. Otherwise the disposition of the animal is the same as that for the high priest, and indicates that the situation is equally serious.

7. The animal required is a male goat, not a bull, and blood is applied only to the main altar. Apart from the burning of the suet and organs, no mention is made of the disposition of the rest of the animal. Traditions do not indicate that it was taken outside the camp, as in the first two cases.

8. Here a female goat or sheep is required, although no explanation is given for not using a male animal. Blood is applied only to the main altar, and, apart from the burning of suet and organs, we learn no more about the disposition of the rest of the animal than we did in 4:26.

9. The only way this makes any sense is to think of communal responsibility—communal dishonoring of God's sanctuary. None of these unintentional sins is trivial, even if only one ordinary Israelite is involved. All these sins involve the entire nation. The authors are convinced of this; they do not need to spell it out.

Section Five: Leviticus 5:1–13

10. Lev 5:1–6 lists four specific examples of actions that in hindsight appeared more serious to those involved. The editors assert that these cases also require purification sacrifices. It is not immediately obvious how one could refuse to be a witness at a hearing or touch an animal carcass or make a rash oath and yet be unaware of these actions.

11. The main similarity between the two passages is that the purification offering serves as a sacrament of atonement. As in several other rituals, provision is made for less expensive offerings of birds or plain flour.

12. These three statements summarize the verses that precede them, thus tying 5:1–13 together, and helping link the entire passage to Lev 4.

Section Six: Leviticus 5:14—6:7

13. Milgrom says that feeling guilt highlights the self-punishment of conscience, the torment of guilt. So the experiencing or feeling of guilt leads to the guilt offering (reparation offering). Feeling guilt leads to the reparation offering, but there are intermediate steps; there might need to be restitution to some third party, or to God and the sanctuary for some sacrilege. Milgrom (345) claims that "in the Priestly demand for remorse and rectification we see the genesis of repentance, the doctrine that will flower into full bloom with Israel's prophets."

14. The basic outline of injustices, restitution, and reparation offering is common to both passages. In Num 5:6 the sin is also described as being unfaithful or committing sacrilege (*myl*) against the LORD. Confessing the sin is specified (Num 5:7), and the atonement offering is presumably the same as the reparation offering of Lev 6, although the word in Num 5 is derived from kpr, the word used in Yom Kippur.

Milgrom assumes that the Num 5 passage is a later summary of Lev 6. The Num 5 passage is more general in style, and adds the note of confession and the case of the injured party dying and leaving no kin who can be compensated. The emphasis on confession may be due to H, the other Priestly school of editors.

15. In 6:1–7 Milgrom notes the process of reclassifying serious sins down to the category of inadvertent sins, as in 5:1–6. Here one commits a sacrilege or an injustice aided by a false oath. If that person later feels guilt, confesses the wrong, makes restitution with the 20 percent added charge, and brings the reparation offering to the sanctuary to gain forgiveness, forgiveness will be granted.

16. Public admission of an injustice, sacrilege, or false oath can bring about ownership of that fault, to use a modern term. Milgrom suggests an analogy with the steps in AA:

> And the confession plays a critical role. It assumes that it takes greater courage to verbalize one's faults to others than just to understand them oneself and that, correspondingly, the ability to confess bespeaks a more resolute desire to alter the status quo. Furthermore, the act of confession assumes the response of forgiveness, human and divine. Thereby the erstwhile isolation (self-imposed) of the alcoholic is by the single stroke of the

confession converted to a supportive relationship: the universe, which has ostracized him (or so he felt), now takes him to its embrace. By the same token, Leviticus also presumes, mutatis mutandis, that the greater effort to articulate one's condition and, if necessary, to make proper amends will effect one's reconciliation with God and man "so that he may be forgiven (6:7)." (375)

Section Seven: Leviticus 6:8–7:38

17. The paragraphs are framed as direct instructions from God to Moses. Yet most references to God in the section are in the third person, except for the first-person references in 6:17 and 7:34, both of which have to do with food portions reserved for the priests.

The main focus is on practicalities regarding sacrifices, and the duties of the priests or of the laity. They range from gestures, management of the fires, disposition of blood and fat, and the allotment of certain hides and portions of meat and grain for the support of the priests and their families.

Clearly the editors felt obliged to review all these details for everyone's benefit. Yet they provided no explanations as to why God wants this or that procedure; nor is there any hint at the possible gradual development of ceremonies by Jewish people themselves. The writers, editors, and their original audiences were all on the same page.

Section Eight: Leviticus 8:1–36

18. These two mentions in Lev 8 of Aaron and his sons serve as a framework to highlight the intervening sacrifices.

19. The phrase *as the LORD commanded (zwh)* Moses appears seven times in this chapter (8:4, 9, 13, 17, 21, 29, 36) as well as seven times each in Exod 39:1–31 and 40:17–38. The frequent use of this refrain (along with related phrases in Lev 8:5, 31, 34, 35) drives home the point that the details of the tabernacle structures and ceremonial furnishings and the elements of priestly office are entirely of divine design. (Scholars now have evidence that some of these details were also customary in other ancient Near Eastern cultures.)

Answers

What is most important is that everyone exposed to the Leviticus traditions (including modern readers) should become aware of all the regulations. This communal awareness promotes a stable understanding of the liturgical year and of the integrity of prayer and worship.

20. In this ceremony, as outlined in Lev 8, the priests-to-be are fairly passive or humble. Moses (perhaps with help) washes them and vests them. Moses offered all the required sacrifices and touched their ears, thumbs, and toes with blood from the ordination ram. He sprinkled blood and oil upon them and upon their vestments. They were under divine command to remain within the outer sanctuary area for the seven days, during which time they took no greater roles than they had on the first day. Nor did they have normal contact with their wives and children during that time. Their food portions from the sacrifices were the same that lay people would have had from well-being or thanksgiving sacrifices. Such passivity was integral to most ancient rituals of passage. God's blessings come only after a period of separation that marks the transition to a new state in life.

Commentators suggest that the holiness required for the priests' sacred responsibilities needed to be augmented or stabilized over that seven-day period. Since they will be so close to the divine realm in their office, they had to be fortified against any hint of impurity or sinfulness.

Christians tend to have their ministers or priests formally commissioned or blessed in sacramental settings which give accent to their individual callings. The main difference is that the ancient Jewish priesthood was a hereditary system, so later generations did not have to repeat the original ceremonies.

21. This is a bit of a trick question. In ancient Israel the sacrifices were performed in silence (once the type of sacrifice had been indicated). This may have been done to distinguish Israel from many other religions where the priests chanted long litanies, spells, and incantations, many of which were taught only to them and not to ordinary worshippers.

Section Nine: Leviticus 9:1–24

22. One modern commentator on Leviticus, Richard Boyce, catches the sense of hope in God and the trust in the form of worship had by the chosen people at this point.

> The Lord is *already* with this people as a cloud, pillar, and abiding presence. What proper worship enables is all the people's *accessibility* to this glory. It provokes a visible sign of an invisible grace, a regular manifestation of a constant reality. When we shun this gift, it threatens not so much *God's* position as *our own*.
>
> Second, deeper even than the desire that God do something for us, is our hunger for God to reveal Godself to us. Over and over in the Scriptures, those who draw closest to God hunger to know God more intimately, to have the light of God's countenance shine upon them, to see God face-to-face. An experience that is usually reserved for only the most intimate of God's partners and, even for them, must be handled in the most delicate fashion (lest they die!) is here made open to all, at the conclusion of a ceremony repeatable in all its details. Worship thus becomes the "regular" means of experiencing the grace of a quite "irregular" God. Though God remains a holy, mysterious, and free Lord, this is not a God who is far off, but near: as near as this week's sacrifices of praise and priestly benedictions. (36)

Milgrom notes that the very notion of burning sacrifices may well have been thought of as a way to transform the offerings into a spiritual dimension. This divine fire in Lev 9 could explain the rule that the altar fires were to be kept lit day and night (Lev 6:2, 12–13). The first offerings were approved by God's fire, so the fire on the altar should never be neglected. Then each subsequent offering could also merit God's approval.

In Lev 9:24 the people *shouted* (*rnn*) and *fell on their faces*. The shouts were probably joyful, and the second phrase usually refers to a prayerful kneeling posture, with head deeply bowed. (An additional verb is used when the kneeling posture is followed by full prostration.) Similar reactions of joy and prayer can be found concerning Samson' parents in Judg 13:19–23, those who witnessed the debate of Elijah and the prophets of Baal in 1 Kgs 18:39, and those with Solomon at the temple in 2 Chr 7:3.

Section Ten: Leviticus 10:1–20

23. The tone of the passage is so matter-of-fact, and God seems to have solved the problem of the unholy fire in so unforgiving a fashion, that it is hard for believers to appreciate how this purging enhances God's holiness and glory, even though he declares that by this episode he has shown

Answers

himself to be holy and to be glorified. The bodies are removed, and Aaron and the other sons are told to continue with the ceremonies. They may not mourn the dead, although the rest of the people may mourn the fact of the burning wrath—a tragedy that had affected the whole sanctuary and all the people.

The unauthorized embers must not have come from the main altar, as specified in Lev 16:12 or Num 16:46. The punishing fire apparently came out of the holy of holies and struck them in the tabernacle courtyard, although it was not the same approving fire that had consumed the offerings in Lev 9:24. The fragment of poetry in 10:3 clearly refers to priests who draw near to the LORD in their roles as leaders of worship.

Despite our unease with these sudden deaths, Milgrom asserts that these two sons "perform the function of sanctifying God—providing awe and respect for his power to all who witness the incident or who will subsequently learn of it." Milgrom (603) cites a medieval rabbi, Abravanel, who explains that ". . . those who serve God more endanger themselves more. Just as those who are closest to the battlefront are more likely to die so those closest in the service of the sanctuary are more prone to err."

Ezek 28:22–23 has a similar notion of God gaining glory in punishing the city of Sidon.

24. Milgrom takes this story as the exact counterpart to the episode of the golden calf. The calf was wrongly made and misused immediately after the covenant at Sinai, and the wrongful censing by Nadab and Abihu took place immediately after God's special approval of the tabernacle rites (9:23–24).

Most scholars take the incident of the golden calf as a creative, emotional profile of the centuries-long struggle to worship only one God. The account of these two sons of Aaron could also be taken as a creative, emotional profile of the centuries long struggle to have small home incense stands eliminated, or at least not misused.

Milgrom calls this polemic in 10:1–7 "a law in story form." P has other case stories—the rebellion of Korah, the transfer of the high priesthood to Eleazar, the deaths of the blasphemer and of the Sabbath stick gatherer. Milgrom (632–33) notes, "law in story form generally has a greater effect upon hearers and readers than apodictic, casuistic or other legal forms: it allows for ready recall of the principles taught and makes principles concrete and easily understandable." He concludes, "for the biblical legislators there was no moral question about the use of story. It was a proper and acceptable mode of legal discourse and teaching. By it they augmented their more abstract teachings to show how in "real life" the principles apply and their breech brings deleterious effects."

25. Having these purification offerings consumed by the priests goes against any sense of demons or evil magic. Real purification is due to God, and the eating of the meat of the animals was a sign that the priests need not fear any independent evil power. The only exceptions were for the inadvertent sins in Lev 4 and the annual purification of the sanctuary on Yom Kippur in Lev 16. In those cases the evil, while not demonic, was too dangerous for the priests to handle or consume.

Milgrom suggests that we think of the priests as embodying purity and life, and the purification offering representing the impurities and death which sin causes. In the eating of the meat, life can be seen to defeat death. While the tabernacle was imagined to collect impurity over the course of a year, the priests themselves did not become impure in the same way, as long as they served faithfully within the sanctuary.

In Lev 11–15 we will see more ritual examples of life defeating death. The priestly traditions in later chapters (often referred to as H, for the Holiness school) will focus on the duty of all people to learn the distinctions and the laws from the priests so that they too could lives of holiness (see 11:43–45; 19:2; 20:7–8, 26, etc.).

26. Most people might see this as a tie, or an honorable compromise.

As noted before, Milgrom respects Moses' right as the lawgiver to challenge Aaron on any point. He sees it as an example of the conflicting roles of prophets and priests throughout several later centuries of Judaism. Moses may have been worried that the burning of this sacrifice might be misunderstood to hint at demonic powers or magic.

Milgrom also admits that when Moses ends his protest, it may represent the Priestly tradition that Aaron had the ultimate responsibility to decide borderline cases such as these.

Another commentator, Stephen Sherwood, is not sure of Moses' resolve at the end of his discussion with Aaron. He notes, "The logic of Aaron's response is difficult to follow. . . . Is the reader meant to infer that Moses accepted a lame excuse and did not press the issue? Would he thereby be compromising on issues that were of vital importance?" (63).

Boyce, on the other hand, admires Moses for seeing the value of Aaron's remarks.

Answers

> Again and again, Moses emerges as a person of singular qualities throughout the stories of Leviticus-Numbers. When zeal is required, Moses has it. When mercy seems necessary, Moses argues for it. Perhaps most difficult of all, when compromise and reversal are in order, Moses is large enough to relent. Rather than Moses betraying a fault of character on such occasions, we may catch a glimpse of one of those characteristics the Scriptures label "divine." . . . Flexibility regarding the rules and procedures by which the Lord is worshiped and served is here seen as a "witness to" rather than a "denial of" the character of God. (38)

Section Eleven: Leviticus 11:1—15:33

27. Some water supplies can be tainted by contact with some unclean animal carcasses, but springs and cisterns are exempt (11:36). Dry seed is also exempt in 11:37. The text does not explain why these exemptions are allowed. Some guess that it would simply be too hard to find alternate large sources of water or seed.

The only verses that provide a motive for following these rules are Lev 11:44–45, reminding us that God wishes us to be holy in imitation of him. God's holiness is mentioned in similar contexts in Exod 22:31; Lev 20:22–26 and Deut 14:21. But this motive is not the same as an explanation for all the classifications of clean and unclean.

28. There seem to be no regulations, aside from the limitations regarding the sanctuary; so the new mother is free to lead a normal, everyday life during this time.

Some guess that the newborn daughter is being considered as a future wife and mother who will also have these serious and minor bleeding episodes, but this is no more than a guess about the eighty day span.

The *atonement* mentioned in those verses seems to refer to the declaration that the mother is now clean. It does not seem to refer to any personal sin, as the term usually does in English.

29. The priest and the person with the skin condition are following rules to judge serious visible symptoms, mainly whitish coloring, surface bleeding, or the spreading of these signs. Some rashes are deemed harmless. Abnormal spots in clothing are judged by similar symptoms, but the color patterns are different.

30. The classifications of clean creatures, the quarantines for new mothers, and the judging of symptoms in skin conditions or clothing are all presented as settled law; we could call them formulas or recipes. The writers assume that the readers understand the reasons behind all this.

31. The three stages of the ceremonies are all after the fact; the serious skin condition has already been cleared up before the ceremonies start. The *atonement* mentioned again in 14:18–20 refers to the declaration of cleanness.

32. We could take these regulations to be hygienic or, more likely, precautionary quasi-religious procedures. In 15:11 the man can stay at home, as long as he washes his hands before touching others. Commentators assume that the same proviso of hand washing should apply to the woman mentioned in 15:19–27.

33. Most non-Jewish readers of these five chapters will likely be swamped and mystified by the welter of details. The initial impression is that we are being presented with a puzzling array of pious customs, some perhaps ancient or more Near Eastern than Israelite, which can contribute to corporate holiness or corporate disrespect for God and his sanctuary over the long run. The restrictions do not seem to be related to personal sins. The inner religious logic of the pious customs is not explained, nor can we find any overarching scientific or medical links among all these cases.

Some animals, birds, and insects may be eaten; *some* illnesses and cases of bodily discharges must be evaluated by the priests for the sake of the community; *some* molds or fungal growths in fabric, wood, or stone must be treated or removed. In many cases the cleansing is fairly simple—a matter of waiting till sunset, bathing, washing clothes, offering small sacrifices at the appropriate time, etc.

34. While we may not pay much attention to a specific prohibition such as this, it does limit the variety of seafood available to people who may not have had the abundance of choices that we have. For example, ancient Israel never developed its own professional class of fishermen. There were few decent streams and rivers under their control, and for many centuries they did not have access to the entire Sea of Galilee. Milgrom cites scientists who claim that the eastern Mediterranean always had much less fish stocks than the western half, although this has improved in recent times (because of the Suez Canal).

So Israel relied on neighboring groups to catch and sell most of the fish the Israelites consumed. Given the meager supplies of fish available, the exclusion of shellfish was a significant restriction. Milgrom argues that this was a deliberate choice, another decision to enhance the reverence for all of God's creatures.

35. Milgrom notes that there have been many theories advanced as to the logic or beliefs behind these quarantines for the mother of a newborn. He argues that the simplest explanation is that the woman's loss of blood is a loss of life forces (as is the man's loss of semen in other circumstances). We noted earlier that ancient peoples were not aware of the almost microscopic ova responsible for conception. The consequent bleeding or loss of some forces of life point to the forces of mortality and death. Jewish faith had eliminated the demonic powers of death found in polytheistic religions, but held to quarantines such as these which abstracted, downgraded, or blurred demonic dimensions without eliminating them altogether. The larger purpose of this downgrading process within Judaism was to highlight God's desire to bless us with his own forces of life and holiness.

36. Milgrom suggests that perhaps Luke, being a Gentile, may have thought that the purification rule covered both husband and wife. Another possibility is that Luke thought of Mary and Jesus himself as coming under the rule, given that in pagan Greek customs the newborn infant had to undergo purification also. In either case the story in Luke focuses on the whole family as a unit, in keeping with the way Jewish families always shared their faith.

37. While the steps are clearly spelled out in this chapter, the symptoms are confusing. Current best guesses are that in addition to psoriasis, 13:30–38 might refer to favus and 13:39 to vitiligo. Many dermatologists argue that none of these chronic skin conditions would improve during the few weeks of quarantines and inspections mentioned. Milgrom suggests the possibility that symptoms of various diseases were conflated as P editors assembled and condensed a complex array of examples of ritual impurities and appropriate ritual remedies throughout Lev 11–15.

38. Lev 14:4 prescribes that the healed person provide the two living wild birds (perhaps sparrows), the cedar twigs, scarlet yarn, and hyssop. The red blood of the one bird, along with the red cedar and red yarn, are

added to fresh water from a running stream or artesian well (the Hebrew phrase is living water). All the images are of the powers of life, which will now drive away the powers of death that were represented by the scale disease. The life forces mixed in the water and the impurity of the disease are transferred by dipping to the second wild bird, which then flies far away. There is a somewhat similar image of evil being winged away in Zech 5:5–11.

Another use of fresh water was for corpse-contamination ceremonies (see Num 19:17). Fresh water is also used in Lev 15:13 for a man to be cleansed after abnormal secretions have stopped. In 2 Kgs 5 the fresh water of the Jordan healed and purified Naaman; here in Lev 14 it only highlights a healing that has already taken place.

Milgrom takes this bird ceremony to be a remnant of an ancient pagan exorcism rite, now modified to be just the initial stage of a complex rite of removal of potential ritual impurity. It seems that the laundering, shaving, and bathing in Lev 14:8 bring about the first state of cleanness, rather than the bird ceremony.

Milgrom is certain that this ancient bird ceremony, now purely symbolic, was retained because of popular demand, indeed as a concession to that popularity. He says that "the people at large demanded it, practiced it, and would not have tolerated its deletion. For them, this rite of exorcism was indispensable" (838).

Roman Catholics and other Christians might understand this popular rite as something like a "sacramental." That is a noun (or substantive adjective) meaning a legitimate simple ritual below the level of the seven sacraments. (Examples could include outdoor processions, the blessing of crops or fishing fleets, placing a crucifix on a living room wall, etc.).

39. On the eighth day the healed person needs still more purification, presumably because he or she can still contaminate by touch.

One male lamb is used for a *guilt offering* (Milgrom calls this a *reparation offering*). The elevation of the entire animal is unusual. Blood from this lamb is put on the right earlobe, thumb, and big toe, and then oil offered at the same time is used the same way. The three sites surely represent the entire body.

A final amount of oil is placed on the healed person's head. The use of the blood in this way marks the passage from the status of unclean to clean, from outcast to fully restored membership. The anointing with oil apparently has the same effect. The ewe lamb will be the *sin offering*

(14:19) (Milgrom calls this a *purification offering*), and the second male lamb will be used as a *burnt offering* (14:19).

Atonement is mentioned at the end of 14:18; this may summarize the entire ceremony, as is implied again in 14:21. We should understand the atonement as precautionary; it may be that the scale-diseased person had done some personal wrong, although that is not likely true in most cases. Further, the sacrifice also cleanses the sanctuary of any possible contamination by people. The burnt offering also provides atonement. Milgrom (858) notes, "The battery of all four expiatory sacrifices—reparation, purification, burnt, and cereal offerings—thereby assures the scale-diseased person that all possible inadvertent misdemeanors have been covered. His wrong is expiated; his disease will not return."

40. Almost all ancient Near Eastern cultures had rules forbidding any sexual relations on the same day as religious ceremonies, often requiring ablutions by both parties. Jewish traditions specified waiting till sundown for full purification to take effect.

One guess for the common hesitation about sexual relations near the time for ceremonies is that the usual loss of fluids could represent the current loss of life forces, even though pregnancies come about this way. Another possible motivation for abstention may have been to express solidarity with everyone else in the worshipping community: the elderly, widowed, incapacitated, children, and infants.

41. Scanning Lev 11–15, Milgrom (1002) sees the lists of what is clean or unclean and what causes ritual impurity (endangering the sanctuary) as "arbitrary and artificial." Many diseases are ignored, while ordinary life experiences of sexual contact, birth, and menstruation are included. The lists "have no intrinsic meaning in themselves but were selected because they serve a larger, overarching purpose." The classifications of the food restrictions in Lev 11 "are also governed by criteria, such as cud chewing and hoof splitting, which are equally arbitrary and meaningless in themselves but serve a larger, extrinsic purpose." The lists of what animals and creatures may be eaten indicate a respect for animal life in general, given humane slaughter and proper disposal of the life blood.

If we consider the human frailties of scale disease, normal and abnormal issues of blood and fluids from men and women, and the proper treatment of the corpses of those recently deceased, what they have in common is death, in a spiritual sense. Death is taken as the opposite of God's life and holiness.

Milgrom (144, 1002–3) concludes, "It is imperative for Israel to control the occurrence of impurity lest it impinge upon the realm of the holy God. The forces pitted against each other in the cosmic struggle are no longer the benevolent and demonic deities who populate the mythologies of Israel's neighbors but the forces of life and death set loose by man himself through his obedience to or defiance of God's commandments."

42. In general commentators do not seem to address this question. The fact that the temple was destroyed in 70 CE also helps to put this sort of question on the back burner. Perhaps some Israelites did not seek too much advice from the priests, although not every skin disease could be hidden under clothing.

We do not know how those quarantined outside home or village kept busy. Some priests who were afflicted with disqualifying blemishes or handicaps were reassigned to tasks that would have rendered them unclean anyway, such as inspecting all the firewood to be used in the temple. Any wood having live larvae or worms within had to be rejected. This chore, however, would not have kept many occupied.

Given what we know of Jewish history, and adding in New Testament stories, it seems that most Jewish people accepted the rules as found in Leviticus and elsewhere. Perhaps those quarantined found it easier to think of the community's relationship to God, whereas we usually tend to think of the individual first. Besides thinking of their communal relationship with God, the quarantined, as part of the whole, represented the effects of the forces of sin that embroiled the whole nation. They would have needed to trust in God's mercy to accept this. As we just heard from Milgrom, these are "the forces of life and death set loose by man himself through his obedience to or defiance of God's commandments."

43. Clearly, de Vaux has grossly oversimplified the faith behind these regulations, instead blaming the priests, rabbis, and Pharisees for a puritanical mindset. In this he may represent the wrongheaded impatience some Christians experience in the face of all these laws. Milgrom claims, to the contrary, that Priestly writers reduced restrictions in many cases, and kept some rituals due to popular demand. I think these laws in Leviticus are a good example of how slowly various doctrines about evil, sin, and ritual change within any religion, and had the temple not been

Answers

destroyed in 70 CE we would have seen more of the lenient trend begun in Leviticus.

Section Twelve: Leviticus 16:1–34

44. In light of all the stress in Lev 10, God's instructions seem very formal, even cold. Aaron may only enter the inner room of the tabernacle wearing certain linen vestments and after having readied several animals for sin or (purification) and burnt offerings. Perhaps the story in Lev 10 is on the back burner, while later, more extensive ceremonies are the concern of the authors at this point.

45. Taking 16:3–10 as a series of understandable components of a long ritual, 16:11 now interrupts the flow and goes back to the sacrifice of the bull and the first goat. We do not return to the Azazel goat until 16:18.

46. If the chapter ended at 16:15, we would assume that using the blood of the bull and the first goat within the holy of holies was the main requirement of the ceremony, and all we would know about the Azazel goat would be what we read in 16:8–10. The point of this question is simply to remind us that all of 16:1–15 presents steps to follow; readers are expected to know why all the steps are necessary.

47. In 16:16 we learn that similar use of the blood is mandated for the outer room of the tent of meeting, but, more importantly, we find out that all uncleanness hampering the sanctuary and all the transgressions and sins repented for by the people of Israel are being forgiven and atoned on this day. This is a much broader claim than anything readers not familiar with Judaism would know beforehand.

48. Putting blood on the horns of the altar (and adding more drops in the seven-fold sprinkling) is another step in the purification of the entire sanctuary. It also *hallows (qdsh)* the altar, as the NRSV has it. The verb qdsh can mean consecrate or, in this context, reconsecrate. Moses did the same at the time of Aaron's ordination (Lev 8:14–15; see also Exod 29:36–37).

One could also think of the altar as the workhorse of the entire sanctuary. The holy of holies was entered by the high priest once a year, and the outer room was used only at specified times. But the altar was used many times every day by priests and Levites, and the people could see it and come near it. It could easily be tainted by inadvertent errors as well as sins. So reconsecrating it annually makes sense.

49. Now that all the parts of the tabernacle and courtyard have been purified, with all the appropriate offerings and sprinklings, the scapegoat is sent on its mission. It is a symbol of the removal of all the ritual uncleanness and guilt for sin.

50. We could say that the ceremony makes sense because God says it does. All of this chapter is presented as direct divine commands to Moses to relay to Aaron. For emphasis, in 16:34 we are reassured that Moses relayed all this as he had been commanded by God.

But one could go beyond thinking of a literal call to obedience. The various uses of vestments, incense, blood, and sacrifice, and even of the scapegoat, function as sacraments. Trust in the effectiveness of sacraments, including the proper human intentions, is found in many religious traditions.

Describing the entire array of steps in detail, including steps only the high priest will perform, contributes to communal understanding and motivation.

51. These burnt offerings simply add to the solemnity of the entire day. Purification and atonement are meant to support adoration as the highest privilege anyone can share.

52. On the most special occasions the animal sacrificed as the sin offering for the high priest or for the entire community bears such burdens that it must be incinerated in a clean place outside the camp to represent the destruction of evil (see 4:11–12, 21; 8:17).

53. The tone of the entire paragraph is that of an everlasting divine decree. The one date each year is mentioned, along with the fact that the people must fast and abstain from all labor. The entire nation must participate, but the specific steps are simply referred to as the atoning actions performed by the high priest.

54. Surely the high priest must have felt awe and humility before God's presence. For this one man, the supervision of the various sacrifices, the burdening and sending away of the scapegoat, and the solitary rites

within the tabernacle were a great responsibility. He alone acted for the sins of the whole nation, including his own inner failings, and he had to set an example of the inner repentance needed by everyone.

By the same token, the one designated to take the scapegoat away probably had many of the same feelings. He, like everyone else, knew all the things the high priest had to do. He could imagine the high priest's privilege of entering the inner room and the holy of holies. Like him, the one tending the scapegoat had significant responsibilities. As he led the goat through the camp (or through Jerusalem), he also had to set an example of seriousness and inner repentance. As he spent the hours alone on the journey he may have thought about all the sins the goat was bearing, and about his strategy for sequestering the goat so that it could never return.

Later rabbis suggested that the goat should be pushed over a cliff, although that is not an integral part of the ceremony. Scholars point out that a domesticated animal would not have lasted long searching for its own food and water, climbing over rocky terrain, or being unaware of the methods of predators. Perhaps the one designated to sequester the animal gave some thought to its fate, a sign of what should happen to sinfulness.

So the high priest in his sacred vestments and the man leading the scapegoat away each had solitary duties for the sake of all the people and for the honor of their most pure and holy God.

Section Thirteen: Leviticus 17:1–16

55. In 17:1–4 we have a straightforward legal standard covering the slaughter of any herd animal by any individual Israelite, although we are not told much about the nature of the sacrifice intended.

In 17:5–7 an explanation is offered (to Moses, to the people, or to us as readers?) that the people of Israel are making idolatrous sacrifices. A clarification is also included, that the mandated sacrifices are *well-being sacrifices*, where most of the meat is returned to the offerer for family use. In these three verses the people seem to be spoken of, not spoken to. Given the clarity of 17:1–4, the repetition at the end of 17:7 that this shall be a statue forever seems superfluous. The people are still being spoken of, not spoken to.

Answers

The phrase at the start of 17:8 could be taken as a resumption of the clear law style that ended in 17:4. The two parts of one speech seem more different than alike; the first part is closer to our own style of law giving.

56. Lev 17:8–9 covers burnt offerings and other sacrifices (but not well-being sacrifices). The two verses seem to be an ordinary liturgical command for a monotheistic community; no explanations are needed or given. The passage concerns itself with the few animals that will be needed for those rites.

57. Lev 17:10 jumps to a different topic: the universal ban on ingesting the blood of animals along with the meat. This well-known ban, already in use, would cover the meat returned to families from well-being offerings or from those and other sacrifices where the priests are given some of the meat. It would also cover the game animals and carcasses discussed later in this chapter.

The ban is simply cited here; it is not being legislated for the first time.

58. Following 17:10, 17:11–12 switches to the second-person plural, and like 17:5–7 offers a summary explanation or clarification for 17:10. The proper use of blood on the altar provides the needed atonement.

Again, we could say that, compared to 17:10, 17:11–12 is more different than alike. Lev 17:10 is cast as the basic law.

59. Lev 17:13 brings up a new topic: permission to hunt wild animals and birds for game for the table. The hunter is simply reminded to drain the blood properly, pouring in on the ground and covering it with earth.

60. We could say that 17:14 undergirds the appropriate draining of the blood as a religious custom in 17:13, or we could say that 17:14 brings a solemn conclusion to all of 17:10–13.

61. The new topic, perhaps unexpected by us, is the permission to eat meat from carcasses of animals that died naturally or from attack by other animals. The brief period of ritual uncleanness incurred is simply removed by bathing, washing garments, and waiting till dusk.

There is no hint here that anyone should decline to use the permission because of the ritual uncleanness that follows.

Answers

62. Both the P and H schools have the religious conviction that non-Jewish resident aliens are truly obligated to observe the ban on eating blood with any meat. They must observe the standard procedure for draining the blood at any slaughter. Indeed the ban obligates all human beings.

What is assumed here, but not explained in detail, is that aliens may join in the practices and worship ceremonies of the monotheistic community of Israel (which I mentioned in answer 56). However, the aliens, like the Israelites, must not offer sacrifices to any other gods (17:8-9).

63. The five references to serious punishments are no more than customary references. We spend no time on whether the punishments eventually are to be implemented by God or by the people, nor on how that will play out. Instead, the main focus of the chapter is on the ban of 17:10 and on the comprehensive law of 17:3-4.

Section Fourteen: Leviticus 18:1-30

64. The opening five verses tie all that follows to God himself; he has made laws to promote life and holiness, and he disapproves of many Egyptian and Canaanite practices. The closing paragraph, 18:24-30, lays out more warnings about the dire consequences of the iniquities and abominations that had been committed by Canaanites and could be committed by Israelites. God's laws are a gift, but they are also a duty. This flows directly from covenant theology.

The two paragraphs could be taken as encouraging, but they also have a no-nonsense tone to them.

65. The laws about incest and other forbidden sexual relationships might seem odd or a bit confusing; one might not be sure if some important relationships have been omitted or assumed. The list might seem a bit long, or one might feel that we do not need to be told to avoid incest with our own mothers or full sisters, etc. Perhaps we need to learn a bit more about ancient family structures in cultures far different from our own.

The editors seem satisfied with their list of cases; they offer few explanations about how these sins might come about, or how to punish those who continue to break these laws.

66. The next five verses, 18:19-23, serve as an appendix, but not a well-organized one. The menstrual taboo is unexplained; avoiding adultery

Answers

with a neighbor's wife, homosexuality, and bestiality might be topics that we as readers find self-evident. The mention of child sacrifice comes as a surprise, although it must have been a Canaanite practice known to the editors and original audiences.

All four sections of this chapter—introduction, laws, appendix, and conclusion—provide an overview of some of God's laws, but the details are kept to a minimum.

67. This itemized overview of some of God's laws is complicated. I have noted that it is mostly a set of warnings, encouraging or no-nonsense in style, at times either too self-evident or not detailed enough. The editors may have had another concern that lies behind and overrides these conflicts in style and organization. They must have had a concern for what it is like in the trenches—that ordinary people were having a hard time living up to patriarchal family customs, living up to a strict monotheism that avoids contact with ancestors and any competing spiritual forces, living up to God's laws and no other. It is not easy to follow the program so easily laid out in 18:5: "You shall keep my statutes and my ordinances; by doing so one shall live; I am the LORD."

Section Fifteen: Leviticus 19:1–37

68. While at first reading 19:2 might sound like a simple piety, in fact it is the theme sentence for the entire chapter. The reference to the Ten Commandments about honoring parents, keeping Sabbaths, and avoiding idolatry and the making of any images, even of God, are ways to be holy. The proper use of meat from well-being sacrifices is the responsibility of the layperson who had it slaughtered and offered at the shrine. Any misuse of the meat on the third day would bring unholiness down on everyone. So 19:3–8 is a partial profile of what it means to become holy.

69. If we take 19:11–12 as further allusions to the Commandments, then 19:9–10 is enveloped before and after by major religious commands. Lev 19:9–10 is an exhortation to allow the poor to glean your fields and vineyards after you have harvested, and have been lenient or bighearted in leaving some significant amount of grain or grapes behind. Lev 19:9–10 is not a major command about worship or justice, but the call to be generous to the poor is enhanced by its surroundings. God is telling us

directly that he is concerned for the poor and the resident aliens, and that we should also share this concern.

70. Stealing, lying, false oaths, fraudulence, disrespect for the blind or deaf (representing the weak), and spreading slander can destroy a nation, large or small. The positive goal must be to promote honesty, respect, justice, and fair business relations all around. Fair business ethics can result in making fewer short-term profits. Helping to build up community involves self-sacrifice; we can't just "let George do it," as the old saying goes.

71. The injunction to love and not hate is a good way to summarize all of 19:3–16. The two verses imply that love will result in positive deeds. One of these deeds at times will be gently but firmly reproving—a task no one enjoys.

72. In building up community, not everyone will make right decisions consistently. Those who notice observable behaviors that pull down morale cannot simply wish that the problem would go away, or simply snub those who are not answering the call to holiness right now. Reproving your neighbor or family member can be a moral necessity, and you cannot be sure in advance that the reproof will be taken in the right way.

73. Lev 19:20–22 stands out from its context and from the whole chapter because it is a case example—most likely a pretty rare case at that. The only other "case" might be 19:5–8 in that there are some specific details there, but most of the chapter is made up of very brief guidelines and exhortations.

Here, the man who has to bring the guilt offering might not be happy about it. If he did not admit his sin until a board of inquiry found him out, he might find it embarrassing to admit all this in public and to the priest at the shrine. Even today many people uncovered in sexual scandals seem more mortified than repentant. But this is a serious issue; the sacrifice is needed to get back on the track to holiness, and holiness is the goal of the entire community. In a way, the board of inquiry administers a reproof, as mentioned in 19:17.

74. While it may not be immediately evident, most of these regulations are meant to combat superstitions or improprieties often associated with polytheism. The proper disposal of the blood of slaughtered animals, proper mourning rituals, and the avoidance of any kind of divination

or attempt to contact ancestral spirits, etc. are all needed to maintain a sound relationship with the one God who is truly holy. Any Israelite use of a superstition or pagan custom that diminishes God's unique role in salvation is a betrayal, and sets the community too close to the rest of the ancient Near East, with all its complex idolatries.

75. Lev 19:34, like 19:18, is a summary, focusing on resident aliens. The love called for did not immediately dissolve the second-class rank of the aliens, but it was a call to treat them humanely. Lev 19:33–37 reminds Israelites that they came from oppressed resident alien stock themselves; they had been aliens in Egypt. God had already loved them back then and brought them to a new land. They must join with God to keep the land holy and worthy of God's choice.

76. The main goal seems to be that if God's people would promote all these virtues and avoid these sins there would be a Utopia of Holiness on earth. People would work well with each other and with nature, the poor and the weak would be supported, and religious ceremonies would be done in unity and sincerity. This Utopia of Holiness would bring us closer to God.

This chapter as a whole was much appreciated by ancient commentators, and a reflective study of it is well worth the effort.

Section Sixteen: Leviticus 20:1–27

77. The call for the death penalty is so strong in these verses that one could assume that the forbidden sacrifices did not last for a long time. On the other hand, the frequent biblical allusions to the problem are taken by commentators to hint at the opposite—that the problem lasted for decades or centuries. The monotheism we associate with Judaism took a long time to develop.

78. The first of the two verses calls on us to consecrate ourselves to holiness. The second has God saying *I sanctify you*. While many readers would likely read both verses as pious exhortations, the question of how God interacts with us for our salvation is always worth considering. It can even be a stumbling block to the faith journey for some people. How can I know and do what God wants if I don't know how and when I am already being helped?

Answers

79. The content is fairly grim. The many marriage prohibitions and penalties are stern, and no one seems to be given a second chance. Adding in the tangential items of cursing parents, or of a man having relations with any woman during her menstrual period, as equally deserving of punishment adds to the grimness. While the death sentence does not seem to apply in 20:17-21, the range of references to being cut off, being subject to punishment, or dying childless still profile an angry God, who will take revenge in different ways.

Every case is presented in black and white. There is no discussion of how to assemble judges or how to take testimony from reliable witnesses. Packing so many death sentences into a few paragraphs can depress modern readers into imagining a grand scale of sin and scandal. To say that the cases were probably rare does not make the depression go away.

80. The shift to noting the importance of eating only clean animals and birds, and of avoiding ground insects, seems odd. Surely the child sacrifices and sexual relations condemned in the chapter are of more weight.

Perhaps the references to dietary laws represent the call by God for his people Israel to be separate in many other ways—more sensitive to the use of animals and birds for food, more sensitive to the grim superstitions polytheism can engender, and more sensitive to the disadvantaged women and children within polygamous cultures.

Section Seventeen: Leviticus 21:1—22:33

81. The wife is not listed, and rabbinic commentators feuded about this omission for centuries. Some note that the word for relatives (*am*) in 21:1 is rather generic, and that the nearest kin in 21:2 are the man's blood relatives (*shar*), which technically do not include the wife. Others recall the passage in Ezek 24:15-18, where Ezekiel was prohibited from mourning for his own wife, who died right after God had given him this stern command. Milgrom sides with those who allow for all the normal rituals by a priest for the death of his wife, noting that Ezekiel was an exception to the rule.

The phrase *as a husband* in 21:4 is not related to this question. It is one suggested translation for an obscure text, and many argue now that the phrase should simply be omitted in translations for technical reasons.

The whole endeavor to ask about the wife is just one example of the hundreds of points in the Old Testament where there seems to be no solution up to this point in time.

82. Obviously the term is an anthropomorphism, a depiction of God in completely human terms (see also Num 28:2). Calling the various sacrifices food for God is not an acceptable or useful theological explanation for any plant or animal offerings within Judaism or most other faiths. The stylism persisted because it does support our concept of God as a person rather than a force, but we must always remember that the personal images we use are very inadequate to the task; they are analogies at best.

83. From the Jewish point of view, everyone gains. The priests follow God's express wishes, and the people get a more worthy set of representatives to mediate the nation's relations with God. The whole nation is encouraged to avoid pagan cults of the dead and of ancestor worship. Young women might have been encouraged to be more worthy of the high standards for being ideal wives.

All this gain is an example of corporate thinking, or corporate spirituality. The profiles may be idealistic, and they ignore some social dimensions of the second-class status of women. No set of detailed regulations, by themselves, can turn humans into angels. On the other hand, having no regulations at all is not a better solution.

84. While some religious groups value simplicity in their rituals, no group promotes a careless or continually amateurish way of worship. Most groups want worship ceremonies done well, as a way to honor the god or gods they adore. We have a phrase for this: "Do it right or don't do it at all."

85. God seems to be cramming in an addendum or adding some footnotes. He assumes that his audience knows all the reasons or logic behind the footnotes.

We might feel removed in time and also in that we don't have much familiarity with the original reasons or logic. But still we get to ponder God's concern for ethics and ritual. Hopefully God is a loving optimist or perfectionist, rather than an irascible, unpredictable fussbudget.

86. We don't normally talk about God *being sanctified*; he is already holy, and is the one who offers sanctification to us.

Answers

The phrase might make more sense if we had a better feel for how 22:31–33 functions as a conclusion for all of Lev 21–22. We will come back to this point at the very end of this Section Seventeen at the front part of the book.

Section Eighteen: Leviticus 23:1–44

87. Lev 23:3 puts the Sabbath at the top of the list of worship ceremonies, but the only component mentioned is the ban on work.

The next verse repeats much of 23:2, and introduces the remaining holy days of the liturgical year. Taking 23:5–8 as an example, we are given many more specific instructions for each event than we received about the Sabbath in 23:3.

88. We have seen this style before. Many of the precise details are mentioned—what to bring and when to bring it. But there is no explanation of why God wants all these instructions followed or of how the ceremony is to help people pray or worship or rejoice or reflect. The editors of the text assume their readers understand all those dimensions.

89. In these directives about the Day of Atonement the style is even more austere. For the only day of fasting each year, with its great emphasis on individual and corporate repentance and purification, we learn of the punishments for not fasting or for working (23:29–30). No other comments are provided about our sins or about God's justice and mercy.

90. In these four verses we learn almost nothing of the festival itself, except for when it starts and ends and the obligation to avoid work on the first and last days.

91. In these verses we are told that Booths is a harvest festival, and that everyone is to rejoice (23:40), using fronds and leafy branches in some fashion. Living in booths is not given much explanation. Were they supposed to make more joyful use of these shelters than their ancestors who had left Egypt and camped this way in the desert? Even the command for everyone to rejoice sounds odd; the command is presented as one more precise detail, when in fact the rejoicing is the whole point.

The story line is that all the words in the chapter are coming from God through Moses to his own people. He and they could have answered this very question for us. But in fact the whole chapter comes from centuries after Moses, and the building of booths is simply set up as a model to be imitated.

Section Nineteen: Leviticus 24:1–23

92. It is easy enough to understand the twelve loaves representing the twelve tribes, but the loaves are not used in any ceremony. They simply remain in the outer room of the tabernacle for one Sabbath week; the incense gets burned, but not the loaves. Perhaps somehow the loaves symbolize the covenantal relationship between the people and God. The fact that they are eventually consumed by the priests does not shed much light on the basic purpose of the symbol.

93. We do learn the Israelite woman's name and tribe, and that her husband was an Egyptian. Her son got into a fight with another man, most likely a full Israelite. It may be that the blasphemer is being depicted as a man of lesser social or religious standing than his opponent. One the other hand, a large mixed crowd had joined the Israelites in their flight from Egypt, and later generations of Israelites allowed resident aliens to live among them. Intermarriage with Canaanites became fairly common, despite official concerns from the priests.

The story is very brief, and does not explain how blasphemy was punished before this case came up. Some speculate that the only technicality was the half-Israelite status of this man, and whether he should receive the same punishment as a full Israelite. So we all wind up waiting for what God will tell Moses in 24:14–16.

94. The death penalty is as stern as it gets. Resident aliens who heard the blasphemy should participate in the execution, and they also risk the death penalty if they themselves blaspheme.

Modern readers can understand the discomfort blasphemy may cause, but would not want to see anyone of any persuasion punished for speaking freely or protesting. Charges of blasphemy can easily be trumped up, and demagogues, religious and especially secular, have manipulated this issue for centuries. We see this as simply a matter of freedom of religion or freedom of speech.

The only way God's directive to Moses makes any sense is as an element of ancient corporate religious thought, which we must examine further.

95. The editors are linking together legal principles about murder, violent injuries, and blasphemy. None of the topics is spelled out at adequate length. There would be much to prove in a court about the level of intent in any case where someone was physically injured or killed. The nature and extent of a blasphemy would also have to be examined carefully.

As in the answer to the previous question, the only way that linking all of these matters together can be fathomed is as an element of ancient corporate religious thought. In Leviticus, as throughout the Pentateuch, faith and justice are always united for the whole nation.

Section Twenty: Leviticus 25:1–55

96. This passage describes fields and vineyards being left alone for a year; they will still provide some food for the farmer and his dependents, but no extra yield is to be harvested or sold. This was a way of returning some minerals and fiber to the soil to increase productivity and aeration. This cyclic system of letting some portions of land lie fallow is still used today in many parts of the world, even though we have modern fertilizers. In Leviticus the system is simply described as part of God's will.

97. The passage is much too short to explain anything. It simply serves as an introduction to much of the rest of the chapter.

98. The cautions to not cheat in transactions simply underline the importance of the system of relating land prices to the time remaining before the next Jubilee year.

99. While ideally we should trust God to provide abundant harvests to manage the Jubilee year's additional rest for the land, the references to storing those harvests are schematic. Some scholars suggest that these verses might have originally been part of an explanation related to the Sabbath year of 25:1–7.

100. These verses return our attention to the property transactions that are also an integral part of the Jubilee year.

101. These twenty-one verses outline methods for helping poor farmers to work off debts at low interest, and to avoid eviction, enslavement, or permanent loss of their land. Those extending credit have to return the lands, and perhaps forgive some debts, at the next Jubilee year. The ones extending credit may break even, but will not make as much profit as in transactions with people not in debt.

102. Lev 25:29–34 is an appendix or perhaps an update to explain transactions with city dwellers (who apparently are not small farmers) and with Levites, who were subsistence farmers in addition to their liturgical duties. The second passage, 25:44–46, is a loophole, allowing for slavery for non-Israelites.

103. These are motivational phrases, reminding the Israelites that in God's eyes they are all resident aliens, tenants, servants, and former slaves whom he brought out of Egypt and to whom he leases all his land. Portraying God's generosity in this majestic way should inspire those in position to extend credit to their poorer countrymen to be equally compassionate and generous. Motivational phrases are often used to promote charity where laws or customs cannot be enforced in any other uniform way.

Section Twenty-One: Leviticus 26:1–46

104. The first two verses focus on avoiding idolatry and keeping the Sabbath, but we could take them as an allusion to or as a recap of all Ten Commandments. The next passage, 26:3–13, imagines great blessings to flow for this loyalty to the Commandments.

105. The wonderful blessings all hinge on the first word in 26:3, *if*. Even though the blessings are conditional, they outline God's love for us, or, more precisely, his generosity. We might consider the extent of the blessings to be idealistic or idyllic; life is never this easy!

106. The range and intensity of these curses should upset the average reader. They are on a par with the gloomy curses of Deut 28:15–68. Lev 26:28 has God say, "I will continue hostile to you in fury." His anger seems out of proportion.

Answers

Traditional explanations do not lessen the shock of reading this passage. We know blessings and curses were stock components in ancient Near Eastern treaties. Thinking of God as the great king who offered the treaty or covenant to start with, commentators note that when kings were enraged everyone gave them the benefit of the doubt. The king's rage was probably justified. We could say that the people seem intent on sinning till the last person dies; perhaps this is a way of describing the people "hitting bottom," to use a modern phrase. Still, none of these explanations is fully satisfactory. One wonders how balanced God could have been in his generosity in 26:3–13 if he becomes so enraged in this passage. There is a graphic verse in Deut 28:63, "And just as the LORD took delight in making you prosperous and numerous, so the LORD will take delight in bringing you to ruin and destruction; you shall be plucked off the land that you are entering to possess."

107. This passage of forgiveness also hinges on the opening phrase in 26:40, *but if*. While the blessings are conditional, the statement in 26:44 is that there should not be utter destruction of the Israelites. God will remember his side of the covenant relationship and wll forgive when they repent. He does not want to destroy everyone; he does not want to terminate the covenant this way.

Still, just as I noted that 26:14–39 can cause us unease about the promises in 26:3–13, I think the same could be said about this closing passage. One wonders how serenely balanced God is in speaking of now remembering covenants *in their favor* (26:45).

All these blessings and curses by God, and all these deep-rooted acts of defiance by Israel, challenge us to trust in God's love and to reflect on our own defiance of his grace.

Bibliography

Boyce, Richard. *Leviticus and Numbers.* Westminster Bible Companion. Louisville: Westminster John Knox, 2008.
Brueggemann, Walter. *Theology of the Old Testament.* Minneapolis: Fortress, 1977.
Green, Alberto R. W. *The Role of Human Sacrifice in the Ancient Near East.* ASOR Dissertation Series. Atlanta: Scholars, 1975.
Levine, Baruch A. *Numbers* 1–20. Anchor Bible 4. New York: Doubleday, 1993.
———. *Numbers* 21–36. Anchor Bible 4A. New York: Doubleday, 2000.
Milgrom, Jacob. *Leviticus* 1–16. Anchor Bible 3. New York: Doubleday, 1991.
———. *Leviticus* 17–22. Anchor Bible 3A. New York: Doubleday, 2000.
———. *Leviticus* 23–27. Anchor Bible 3B. New York: Doubleday, 2001.
Miller, William T. *The Book of Exodus.* Question by Question Bible Study Commentary. Mahwah, NJ: Paulist, 2009.
———. *The Book of Genesis.* Question by Question Bible Study Commentary. Mahwah, NJ: Paulist, 2006.
———. *A Compact Study of Numbers.* Eugene, OR: Wipf & Stock, 2013.
Sanders, E. P. *Judaism: Practice and Belief, 63 BCE–66 CE.* Philadelphia: Trinity, 1992.
Sherwood, Stephen K. *Leviticus, Numbers, Deuteronomy.* Berit Olam. Collegeville, MN: Liturgical, 2002.
Vaux, Roland de. *Ancient Israel.* New York: McGraw-Hill, 1965.

www.ingramcontent.com/pod-product-compliance
Lightning Source LLC
Chambersburg PA
CBHW070317230426
43663CB00011B/2158